The Drownt Boy

The Drownt Boy
An Ozark Tale

Art Homer

University of Missouri Press
Columbia and London

Library of Congress Cataloging-in-Publication Data

Homer, Art.
    The drownt boy : an Ozark tale / Art Homer.
        p. cm.
    ISBN 0-8262-0981-5
    1. Homer, Art—Homes and haunts—Ozark Mountains
Region.   2. Ozark Mountains Region—Social life and
customs.   3. Ellington (Mo.)—Social life and customs.
4. Poets, American—20th century—Biography.   5. Homer,
Art—Childhood and youth.   I. Title.
PS3558.04466Z467 1994
811'.54—dc20
    [B]   94-27560
                                                      CIP

Designer: Stephanie Foley
Typesetter: Connell-Zeko Type & Graphics
Printer and binder: Thomson-Shore, Inc.
Typeface: Galliard

For acknowledgments, see the last printed page of this book.

To my family—

*Robert Homer, Colleen Davidson,
Dennis Mahoney, Alison Wilson, David Homer,
Amy Mahoney, Willow Homer, Myfanwy Smolsky,
Remus Smolsky, and Alexis Lindsay.*

Contents

The Drownt Boy

Magic

I WASN'T BORN IN A LOG CABIN. Friends accuse me of this curiously American origin, but I can't boast the distinction. My birth certificate shows my place of birth as Carter's Medical Clinic, Ellington, Missouri. My parents brought me home to a log cabin twenty miles north on a red dirt road through second-growth oak-hickory and pine forest.

You can still drive this road, if you can find it, past small frame houses, white, with tin roofs, becoming fewer and farther from the road as you leave the town behind—can still drive through redbud, sassafras, and dogwood at roadside, giving way to oak, maple, juniper, and on certain slopes large stands of yellow pine unexpectedly cool. Chambers of light open in the wall of trees where former homesteads stood—some of them my relatives'. Turkeys may dart in front of you. Certainly the large box turtles will be out if it is summer. Deer are plentiful, and so were half-wild cattle and hogs when I was a child and the hills were open range. Breathe deeply and the hardwood forest with extensive stands of pine reminds you that John Muir savored the Sierra forests for their variety of aromas and tonics. The Ozarks are also diverse in wildlife. The rivers hold sixty to ninety species of fish, depending upon how many separate minnows you distinguish.

The road evolved from an abandoned railroad right-of-way when

1

my father was a young man. Previously, backwoods folks took their mule-drawn wagons on the logging access road across marsh and up steep grades. Traces of it still run through the hills, overgrown now. The "nigh cut" they called any such forest track—even if it was longer than the high road. People still hauled corn and cane to town in wagons when I was a child in the midfifties. The Depression moved into the Ozarks, liked it, and retired there after World War II, letting the rest of the country go on with the boom times.

The place was bypassed for geological ages. The landscape is part of the Appalachian uplift separated from its parent by the fault under the Missouri-Mississippi valleys. Rivers running through the broken peneplain are literally older than the hills. They once ran through plains that sank under seas, then lifted, submerged, and rose again. Now the plateau is broken and eroded into hills and steep hollows, the rocks softened and crumbly from erosion. The rivers retain the meanders of plains rivers, though hills have risen and half collapsed around them. The rocks are old: sandstone dissolving around granite knobs, limestone from sea creatures, flinty chips of chert working up through plowed fields with the frost heave. And the forest is old, a crossroads of geology, of plant and animal life from the eastern woodlands and the western plains. Southern riparian species homestead river bottoms. Northern ferns forced south by the Wisconsin ice sheet survive in the mouths of caves and in cool spring branches hundreds of miles from their current range.

A crossroads of peoples too. Here, the unimposing Bluff Dweller looked down on the Hopewell-Mississippian city states along the river. Centuries later, guerrilla warfare of the Civil War brought first one side then the other ferrying their wounded to Hospital Cave in johnboats. The James Gang rode through, leaving a bullet hole in one of the log uprights of the Centerville Post Office—which, by the time I saw it, was worn smooth and round from generations of boys sticking their fingers into it. I imagine men my grandfather's age getting splinters.

What I have to say about the place is no truer than the claim my friends make of my birth. "You'd argue with a signpost and go the wrong way," my mother says. A combination of childhood memory, history, and wishful thinking, my research has been haphazard. The bullet hole, for instance, could be a clerk's joke at the expense of small boys. The Post Office is absent from current guidebooks of the place. No one remembers it. I may be remembering the wrong town.

Then again, no one remembers the old tram road past my folks' place. Visiting Ellington a few years ago, I asked directions at a supermarket. A country gospel group performed from a flatbed trailer in the parking lot. I remembered clearly where the curving low-water bridge used to sit under two feet of water at flood. My uncle, the bus driver, traversed it in low gear, water climbing bus steps, he finding the curve by memory. The clerk had lived in the town all her life and didn't remember the bridge or the road. She knew the half-surviving town of Corridon at its opposite end, a forty-mile drive by the state highway instead of twenty over the old right-of-way. The stock boy, she said, had "taken that hot rod of his over all the back roads in the county." He could tell me where to find it if anybody could.

He did.

The low-water bridge was gone, the road reached by a turnoff the other side of county bridge sixteen. I didn't recognize the first three miles of the tram road under its curious paving. The calico asphalt of varying age and composition looked like excess from highway projects rolled out when the heavy equipment operators got around to it. Soon, however, it turned red rock and clay, leveled monthly by the county grader—down in the morning, back twenty miles that afternoon. Across these ridges the school bus had carried me, a backwoods kid, into a town of sophisticates with running water and electricity. Seventeen miles to Ellington, three and a half to the village of Corridon, towns most kids in the fifties would have considered irredeemably hicksville. At night I took the road back, way, way back into the woods. Back into the past and into magic.

That the woods mean magic I had always taken as personal mythology—finding the submerged road by memory—until I began
reading nature writers. Now I can construct a veneer of scientific
backing for my beliefs. Most chroniclers of natural history portray the
plains as the place where progress happens. In "How Flowers Changed
the World," Loren Eiseley explains that evolving plants and insects of
the plains literally prepared the ground for increasingly sophisticated
animals. Some of these crept back into the forests. Magic has nothing
to do with progress. Ecologist Paul Shepard, in his *Thinking Animals*,
gives a riveting account of the evolution of intelligence, important
segments of which happened in the plains. As Shepard describes it,
"The intelligence of mammals and insects and birds is the mind of the
grassland" whereas "trees are comparatively shallow beings and the
earth beneath them a cool veneer."

If progress is necessary to evolution, however, so is escape—if
memory, also forgetting. Shepard does credit the forest with a role in
the evolution of intelligence. When our mammal ancestors were driven
back under the trees, their vision-centered intelligence had to use the
hearing centers of the brain to adapt to a limited horizon and nocturnal habits. Out of such marginal forebears and forced connections
intelligence arose.

Similarly, marginal peoples retreat to the forest. Theirs is a journey
backward in time, be their forest the oak groves of Europe, the rain
forest of the Tasaday, or Appalachian hollows. Abandoned in this
journey are not only the rewards of technological progress but some
of the assumptions of postindustrial, postmodern society. These assumptions—for better *and* for worse—are forced into connection
with older postulates about the world.

If our rational vision of the world has given us principles with
which to control our surroundings—to predict the future and avoid
some of the consequences of time's one-way arrow—perhaps some of
the older, magical visions better prepare us to accept the present in all
of its contradictions. This divination is not a foretelling, but a telling,

a way of casting and recasting experience to give it meaning in terms apprehensible to the heart, however painful that may be. We can then accept consequence, can truly be con-sequent—following together. For a moment, time's arrow points toward us, the present, from all directions.

The Ozarks remained, if not retrograde, at least untouched by progress until the census crews, and the lumber and lead-mining companies, took notice at the turn of the century. They discovered people still living the frontier life on old homesteads, hunting, subsistence farming, curing with herbs, and open ranging. Old Scottish tunes retained their original forms. So did the language, as well as various social structures from Scotland, Ireland, England, and later Germany and Russia. The church clung to the splintery cross of its early Protestant dourness, but it wasn't standing still. Even Calvinism devolved enough to coexist with root doctors, snake handlers, and who knows what kinds of African and southern po'-white, holy rolling, shout-your-hair-down practices. Secluded as the Vietnam vets who hid in the Olympic rain forest, as the forgotten Japanese soldier on his jungle island, the Ozarkians were retreating in time, the forest working its charm on them.

My first memories are not of the Ozarks, but of St. Louis. When my parents went there for work, they alternately left me in my Grandmother Homer's care or took me along. Such memories blend with my mother's stories, and both deny the black-and-white photos. The towheads in them could not possibly be my brother and me. We stare moonfaced over a birthday cake, lean against the cabin. Here we are behind the chair in which we got our haircuts, now in front of the Model T with the crank dangling from the radiator. I remember curbs, a two year old's tiredness at the hard sidewalks and new hard-soled shoes. Mother and Aunt Helen, or Mother and Father, lift me by my arms up and down the city's curbs—*Wheeee!*—trying to make a game of it, but I wasn't buying it. This is corroborated by photos of me in an honest-to-god Buster Brown suit, standing between my parents—the archetypal little man fighting to separate mother earth and father sky. They're still happy. I frown like trouble waiting to happen.

We soon returned to the cabin of two rooms, living room and kitchen. Our eighty acres of forest had less than five acres cleared. Sumac reclaimed a grazing field on the access road, and a couple of acres surrounded the cabin. The yard sat on a knoll, native grass on the north side, plowed garden on the south. From the gate at the turnaround, ending a mile of access road, a well-defined dusty path ran to the door. Later, the addition on the north of the cabin added a bedroom and a living room with picture windows. Father scythed the grass and raked it by hand, and we fed it to whatever stock happened to be about, either ours or unclaimed. Later, we moved to Ellington twice for my father to find work, but returned, me happily, to the cabin each time.

Fortunately for my personal mythology, reforestation programs and national park expansion have reestablished pine stands and aided the natural succession. The forest has outgrown my memory of it. Not easy. Living in a log cabin is like living inside a tree. Ours was local second-growth pine, crosscut, the knotholes axed down more or less smooth, the corner joints hand chiseled and lock notched with extended corners. The logs warped, and the gaps between them needed constant chinking. The sills and floor joists rested on rock pilings, so settling and leveling was synchronous with the land. The house rotated slightly on its foundations in one strong storm—not uncommon in what is still tornado country, despite its relatively high relief. And nature lives with you. For chinking will not keep out animals. I had to convince my mother the banded snake crawling on the rafters was a coral snake, not its innocuous mimic, the king snake. The encyclopedia was on my side—black and red bands separated by yellow borders. I had sighted a semitropical snake in a temperate climate. No wonder it wanted to move inside; the nights were cold.

My mother warned me there could be snakes and who knows what under the house. I thought it would be safe, however, since my dog made her home down there, and crawled after her. I kept a sharp lookout. My mother walked above me in the kitchen. I crawled along on my back, the dirt like lowering sky above my head. The bottom of the floor was all the more alien for being upside down. My mother dropped something and yelled. A pale body washed across the bark of the rough-hewn joist, crossed down into the dirt, and coiled in a scrape the dog dug to escape the heat. I didn't want to call out. I was thankful when the dog quietly came and ate the white-bellied coil— actually, lapped it up. Like a slide projection suddenly brought into focus, the snake resolved itself into a pool of milk, spilled between the floorboards, along the joist, and into the dirt. The dog capitalized on my mother's accident.

Other guests were more a danger to themselves. In the half-finished addition, the picture window gaped unglazed for weeks. Two smaller windows on the side walls had frames and panes. Hummingbirds barreled in the opening and tried to leave through the glass. They buzzed the panes like flies. We had to catch them and rush them outside quickly before they exhausted themselves. If we held them long, fright killed them. Each nearly weightless body was a soft palpitation punctuated with the light scratch of claws as it discharged itself into the air.

Our house was one danger, our pets another. One of the cats killed a bobwhite, the quail whose self-naming call is ubiquitous along fields and riverbanks. My parents looked for the orphan chicks in the tall grass of our yard, homing in on their peeps—not yet the whistle of the adult. It was late and we needed to find them before dark, when either wild animals or our pets would quickly finish them. My brother and I sat amused by our parents' exaggerated care, walking through the tall grass. Despite their best efforts, one voice after another stilled and they found the remains on their shoes. The perfectly camouflaged chicks will freeze even if they're crushed. As juveniles, they grow feathers enough to explode from under your foot into the roar of flight that makes quail hunting so exciting.

Not primeval, the Ozarks, but primal—a first step out of reason's merciless light and back into the liquid motion of shadows under branches. What the nineteenth-century scientists referred to as Nature's profligacy was my affluence. A more directed teacher might have presented the ant as ample demonstration that the six-legged exoskeleton was a viable anatomical design. Then I could have learned the happy word *cooperation* as I watched the social structure of the hive. Instead, I continued to watch bugs willy-nilly: termite; walking stick; the clickbug whose hard, jointed body squirts from your fingers like a watermelon seed when he "clicks" his joint; dung beetle; ladybug; the leafy katydid; praying mantis (the wonderful pun of her pious stance, the body of her prey broken before her); milkweed butterfly emerging from the cocoon; potato beetle and its soft grub. Then, in no particular sequence: reptiles, amphibians, birds, mammals, and, always, the column trees, those first and most universal caryatids. These were my daily companions. Because we subsisted on a nearly equal level with these, our prey, our predators, and our competitors for hard-won food, a part of my experience would be forever strange to my generally urbanized generation—even to kids from the increasingly domesticated, industrialized farms of more prosperous areas.

We were backward—not anachronistic, but anti-chronistic, half feral by some standards. Like the novelist's character living a flashback to develop the plot, like the equations of the astrophysicist studying ever more distant and ancient sources of light from the big bang, like the computer models linking modern genetic patterns to fossil DNA, we existed with the arrow of time inverted. We were like T. H. White's wonderful conception of Merlin living reversed in time, whom the young Arthur meets (not coincidentally in the forest) weeping in farewell to his longtime friend from the perspective of his anti-chronological progress (egress?) toward birth. Who were his contemporaries? Who are mine?

Come here,
Motherless Sparrows
And play
with me.

Thus wrote Issa, the sixteenth-century Japanese Haiku master, at age six. Like him, I sometimes preferred my forest playmates: birds, bugs, and snakes. Lizards were my pets for a day. The blue bellies' tails detach, flipping like baby snakes to distract the bird or young boy who grasps the tip of one. They rode my shoulder leashed with a string around my top shirt button. They would not be fed. Not herbivores, as a few experiments with lettuce showed, they had no interest in dead or stunned flies. They suffered no ill effects from my handling. Once captured they adjusted by sleeping, keeping one double-lidded eye open for escape, and conserving energy. My frenetic metabolism put out enough heat for both of us. At school or church functions, boys dashed them against rocks or logs to kill them. I killed one. It lay on its back, its hands slowly curling up, its gesture less a plea than a question. "Why?"

I knew the motion was reflex—like a headless chicken's flapping. I had seen birds drop dead lizards in the dirt at my approach. Even minus a head, their feet curled up in this ineffectual gesture. I was not squeamish about dead things and would analyze—literally, "take apart"—whatever I found inside strange skin. These older boys had no interest in this, had probably seen as I had the silvery flesh, the amazingly small amount of blood, the translucent bones. Shrikes, or "butcher birds," impale lizards on thorns and barbwire fences. Even this, the victim alive, impaled and left to age in hot sun, serves a purpose. My parents killed for food—chickens, a pig—but they made my brother hold the houseplants he had broken until he could hear them cry. It didn't take long. Subsistence hunters, human or animal, are opportunistic feeders, neither amused nor revolted by the dirty but necessary work of killing.

The lizard was a hunter too. I must have spent hours watching lizards and frogs hunt, though I whined about being bored. My mother's response was "Glad to meet you, Mr. Board. I'm Hammer N. Nails," sticking a finger in my arm and pounding it in with her other hand. The louder my whining, the harder the "nail" got pounded. I must have had a modicum of patience, however. I remember watching frogs catch dragonflies—the impossible speed, the moment of the hit frozen in my mind, a wing or tail protruding oddly from the mouth—and wondering whether the frog's tongue or its bite killed. With patience, I could also watch stalkings the world usually allows to remain hidden.

Watching on a slant through the unfinished window in the addition, my chin braced on the sill, I could see high cirrus stalk the horizon. Fighting drowse at afternoon nap, one could pretend to sleep, watch the minute hand stalk the hour hand, and contemplate the tortoise and the hare. This would have been the key-wound captain's clock. We had no electricity. The hands moved slower even than the praying mantis, a pendulum hypnotizing its prey with its swaying. The clock hands were like the mantis in another way. When the minute hand got close enough, the last increment of distance disappeared in a quantum lunge. First the two hands were apart by ever so little, then they were not. Then the dragonfly was only parts prying the frog mouth into a gloating mow. The mantis dismantled its struggling catch in small bits, a dainty spinster with corn on the cob, the misdirecting wings folded like a napkin. Then the frog again, a grasshopper leg kicking until it came off, dropped on the ground, still jerking, lizard tail, my mother shaking me, chiding me for falling asleep so quickly, my nap over and the sun slanting orange through the south window.

This is how time passed. Ample to realize the mysteries of eating and dying. First for young boys is eating. Some troubled children ate dirt, according to my mother. Perhaps one could cut out the middlemen—the animals, the plants—keep hand-over-handing it down the food chain. Plants grew from dirt. Forest dirt was mostly leaf matter mixed with sticks and sand that feels like boulders in the mouth. Dig below the duff and leaf mold, and mineral dirt will give you an actual taste of the land. The nauseating aftertaste I recognized years later when someone talked me into chewing a zinc tablet as a cold remedy. I found clay bland and palatable. Though aluminum-foil generations would doubt it, good clayey mud is perfect for baking potatoes, keeps the heat in as well, and the moisture better. It crumbles off, and you don't have to pack it out. If you're hungry enough, you can eat it to keep hunger pangs away.

. That's what those children were doing, what many poor children in the rural South did and probably still do. Eat clay. There's plenty of it. Certain kinds of clay help fight food poisoning and decrease the bitterness of acorns and other food. Other clays, kaolinites, provide anti-diarrhetics and fillers in diet food. Geophagy and other vices of the poor are acquired tastes, but unlike more sophisticated appetites, they are rarely conceived out of boredom.

Despite my protests, a child's ill temper, it was hard to be bored. Afternoons I conducted original research into the nature of time and its relationship to food. I had facilities that would be the envy of many a scientist. Poor we may have been, if not reduced to eating clay for lunch, but we had books. Books and kerosene lights for reading at night, an upright piano, a windup Victrola with records from Caruso to Tin Pan Alley songs. A wooden, string-jointed Mr. Tambo attached to the spindle and did a minstrel dance. Our radio lit up with mirror-topped vacuum tubes and had a tone that would drive a blues guitarist crazy. It ran on a wet cell the size of a motorcycle battery. On monthly trips to Ellington, we left it at the service station to be recharged. With rationing, the charge would last all month. Bible readings gave way one night a week to Grand Ole Opry direct from Nashville, now clear as a movie sound track, moments later wavery with distance, as storms, chance disturbances of the ionosphere, or a variation in the battery's output disturbed the signal.

Everything from a piano to encyclopedias was at my disposal if thunderstorms or the palpably malevolent heat kept me indoors. Secondary sources didn't interest me when I could get out and about my field work, my watching and smelling and tasting. With luck, the gods would give me "a day worth all the rest."

One such day I followed lines of flying ants back to their hive, a rotten stump. Stumps with hollow centers collect pools of "spunk-water," highly recommended by root men for boils, warts, and skin problems of all sorts. For years after the tree is cut, it sends up watershoots. Later, they decay, forming soft mounds for ants to inhabit. The forest was an ink-wash background of limbs, highlighted with buds and blossoms. The ants danced across it like blown petals. For a while I didn't notice the creature sitting atop the stump like a miniature dragon. Sharp scales ratcheted out from the neck in a ruff and out along the back and sides, each a knife stroke clear and definite as the lines of Edo period prints, as if the outline of scales against background gray were all that held this creature together. I remember creeping slowly closer until the blue underbelly became visible. This color, when I saw it years later in the famous views of Mt. Fuji, suddenly reminded me of the incident.

What turned out to be a blue-bellied (or six-lined) lizard sat on the ant stump, tongue mechanically flicking up squadrons of the flying ants as they emerged from their holes. So bloated was the metallic reptile skin that the blue coloring frosted with expansion like paint on an inflated balloon. Along the sides and back the scales stood on end like Samurai armor.

The Ozarks are good habitat for reptiles, amphibians, and insects. Nights overflow with a chorus of tree frogs, insects, and birds. Some have names little boys can't understand. If Katy did, why whip poor Will? Others have no name. Some call in voices like chain saws starting up, the voices of the aliens in the radio version of *War of the Worlds*. The walk across the pasture to the outhouse resounded with such voices. The background calls of whippoorwills answered the cries of wills more distant, and farther yet, till one could hear echoes of infinity, the universe expanding like Dante's Paradise, voice to voice—each voice flying away from the other until in some red-shift each went beyond the range of perception and silence fell among the blackness. Even the insect prey of these whiskery nightjars fell silent at these times. I turned and raced through the head-high milkweed for home, clutching my crotch. I had heard the wills called natural watchdogs, their silence a sure sign of approaching danger. No amount of reason could convince me they were being silent on my account.

Children who roam the woods understand the food chain early. Lizards ate insects, birds ate lizards, I ate birds, and somewhere, probably out on the way to the outhouse, something would eat me. Every day, dung beetles rolled their Sisyphean burdens up the dusty path. Though it wasn't our droppings they were neatly bundling up, it may as well have been. Everything recycled. I was proving an axiom: the animals at the top of the food chain are more timid than their prey. The bobcat is more furtive than the squirrel or rabbit, having eaten so many that a complete rodent of fear resides within its heart. It understands and uses the prey's fear against it. Like other predators, I sat uneasily in my precarious niche. Such inductive reasoning comes easily to children, however unconsciously. I had thousands of specific instances from which to build a general theory.

What I think of as magic comes from this, I think: induction. In both senses of the word. First, the magical in art or in culture is a way of seeing the world. Sympathetic magic perceives the affinity between two things (spunkwater and rejuvenation), without looking for cause—without an "irritable reaching after fact and reason," to quote Keats. Magic happens because trees fall in the forest with no Cartesians to ponder them. By deductive standards, if there is one person in the forest, there is still no corroboration. Skepticism stands one in poor stead. *On* the plains the tribe huddles together. *In* the forest, the individual is primary.

Yet one never stands alone. The hypothetical question is flawed by definition. *In the forest,* it is impossible for a tree to fall with no one to hear it because a forest is a community. A forest, Thoreau proved in his address to the farmers of Concord, cannot get on about its business without the squirrels. The same goes for the insects, gastropods, and what have you. For millions of years humankind itself has been shaping the forest—planting, clearing, burning underbrush for better hunting. Besides its arrogance, the question betrays an ignorance of the language of trees.

Tree language uses the second kind of induction, also essential to magic, the more or less physical business described in the Tenth Edition of *Merriam-Webster's Collegiate Dictionary:* "the process by which an electrical conductor becomes electrified when near a charged body, by which a magnetizable body becomes magnetized when in a magnetic field or in the magnetic flux set up by a magnetomotive force, or by which an electromotive force is produced." Asking exactly what that process *is* is likely to leave one as thoroughly flummoxed as asking a shaman about the "forces," "fluxes," and "fields" of spirit power. Let's try another example: "the sum of the processes by which the fate of embryonic cells is determined and morphogenetic differentiation brought about." Good God! The fate of embryonic cells. What happens is that something happens. The cells line up like steel shavings over a magnet. The biologist, the information-science theorist, and the third grader all ask the same question: How do they know to do that? Their only answer is the etymology of the word *induce* (in- + *ducere,* to lead). They don't know. They are led to it, induced, "brought forward"—another definition of the word. Then does the field *know?* the forest *hear?*

A blight strikes the edge of the wood. Dying trees produce chemical compounds and electrical pulses thought to be "messages." Scientists find no mechanism by which trees on the opposite edge of the wood could receive or understand such messages. Nevertheless, they adapt before the blight arrives. Perhaps complex molecules are "inhaled" by the tree's respiratory system; perhaps hair-thin roots pick up magneto-electric fluxes. "All hear, all hear. Yellow pine felled by blight." This is why trees don't bear philosophical chestnuts.

So, in what was as lively a community as any big-city neighborhood, I was picking up messages too. The word on the street was a bit more universal than the old saw of a syllogism on Plato's mortality. Things die and eat and live and change. Frogs from pollywogs eat insects— either on the wing or as mosquito wigglers—and are eaten by snakes. Lizards become dragons when they eat ants that fly like mayflies, though when the ants walk, lizards seldom bother them. Everything— dung, dead trees, and pets, live butterflies and baby birds, acorns on the ground, spilt milk, the dirt—is food for whatever can stomach it.

Living in and of the forest, it is hard not to see the motive force of the universe as magic, a net of reactions that follow their orderly patterns simply because those patterns exist. The universe leads itself along by its bootstraps: induction. William Blake: *To generalize is to be a fool.* Walt Whitman: *To elaborate is no avail, learned and unlearned feel that it is so.*

Deduction, on the other hand, promises wealth through the application of easily grasped principles. Wealth—of information, money, food surpluses—gives us power over the world. Without power, the attraction fades. We are left with the habit of seeing what we expect to see. If we are to attain higher aims—celebration (art), sustenance (hunting-gathering), or knowledge (religion, pure science)—we must overcome this experience-shaping process of deduction. A fat white-tail buck takes several bounds with the flag of his tail up. The hunter's eye (human? cat?) draws a line connecting the dots of each bound toward where she expects the fourth to appear. The deer simply tucks his tail, changes direction, walks a few steps into the background pattern of the forest, and, from the hunter's perspective, disappears.

An art teacher took her class into a public park to paint elm trees. On their boards, familiar shapes began to appear. Mixing a tree-bark brown, the students laboriously sketched in the outlines of limbs, leaving white lacunae where green brush strokes would represent clustered foliage. When the instructor had looked at these, she asked one particularly meticulous student to touch the color brown on the tree trunk. The student treated it like a trick question, but the instructor assured him that she really wanted him to try. The student's confusion increased. He appeared unable to perform this simple act. His confusion reminded me of the neurologists' reports on the victims of brain injury. Somehow, putting the idea into action was too much for him.

Finally, as if a light had been turned on, he said "I can't. There isn't any brown." The instructor then had the rest of the class turn to their paintings. Most of them were brown. What were they painting? Certainly not elms, gray-barked, with perhaps white splotches of lichen and green moss. Their model is indigenous only to kindergarten coloring books. Vaguely deciduous with brown trunk and cloudlike green crown, this tree casts no shadow and drops no twigs on primary green grass under a yellow spider sun.

Whatever sleight of hand the magician shows us is only prelude to the wonders we will see if we abandon our complacency long enough to re-envision the world, to see it in others of the ways it is. Seeing the world anew, no matter how stifling we find our old perspective, is difficult. It often requires ridiculous postures. Van Gogh wrote his brother that he could see more clearly through his eyelashes— squinting at the world. Thoreau favored looking backward between his legs to stand the world on its head. When all else fails, we must steal perspective from children.

"Daddy, how does the moon get inside the clouds?" My daughter must have been about five. (My daughter Willow—I'm serious about this tree business.)

"Well, it just looks like that. See, the moon [I make a fist and hold it over my head] is way up here. Okay?"

Willow nods.

"And we're way down here." I point at my feet.

Another nod.

"And the clouds are in between." I wiggle my fingers at waist level, conscious of the violence I'm doing to scale. "So you see that the moon can't really be inside the clouds."

"Sure it is. Look!"

I'd read Bashō. I'd read Spock. I knew when I was outmaneuvered. "Okay, you tell me. How does the moon get inside the clouds?"

"It blooms in."

"Blooms? I'm not sure I understand?" Getting cagey here, I employed a bit of Socratic technique.

"Sure. You know how a flower blooms *out*?" Using her hands to demonstrate.

"Uh-huh."

Willow reverses the hand motion. "Well, the moon just sort of blooms *in*."

"Okay, Honey. Daddy's got to go home and write now."

Zen Mind, Beginner's Mind is the title of a book by Shunryu Suzuki. The title is the premise. When we wish for a child's vision of the world, we are wishing for the oldest one. When a child sees a forest as a city of animals, isn't it simply reversing the process that led to the building of the city? Wouldn't it be natural for city builders who have moved to the floodplains, or cleared the forests for extensive fields, to re-create the lookout tree, their cover, the myriad trails of the forest when they build their walls and towers and labyrinths of streets?

Augustine characterized the city of man as motivated by self-love, the city of God by love of God. Certainly, "the study of man" has proven tautological. "Self contemplation is a curse," says Theodore Roethke, "that makes an old confusion worse." We look back to the forest. Even those quintessential plains dwellers, the Sioux, recognized the center of their nation's hoop, the intersection between the red and black roads, as a tree. Lured from their ancestral forest by the promise of horse power, they kept much of their eastern woodland ritual. The horse Indians of the Pampas did the same. In *Voyage of the Beagle* Darwin reports:

> Shortly after passing the first spring we came in sight of a famous tree, which the Indians reverence as the altar of Walleechu. . . . As soon as a tribe of Indians come in sight of it, they offer their adorations by loud shouts. . . . Being winter, the tree had no leaves, but in their place numberless threads, by which the various offerings, such as cigars, bread, meat, pieces of cloth, &c. had been suspended. Poor Indians, not having anything better, only pull a thread out of their ponchos, and fasten it to the tree. Richer Indians are accustomed to pour spirits and maté into a certain hole, and likewise to smoke upwards, thinking thus to afford all possible gratification to Walleechu.

Darwin, empathetic as always, is a hundred years ahead of his time in anthropology, reporting, "The Gauchos think that the Indians consider the tree as the god itself; but it seems far more probable, that they regard it as the altar."

At the center of my Ozark world was a hole where offerings were made. The god of this place was present, for I could see my offerings devoured. I called it doodlebug. Known as an ant lion, it was the larva of a small fly (*Myrmeleon*) that made a whirlpool of sand or dust by crawling backward in the loose medium until it had excavated a conical pit with its large jaws at the base. Insects, mostly ants, blundered into the pit and disappeared, sifted through into a gateway out of this life. Abandon hope.

Behind the cabin, a ten-foot-deep pit in the red clay held frogs and water, sometimes in near-equal proportion. This, I explain to my urban friends, was our cistern, a container or reservoir for capturing rainwater. A stringy old man had water witched the cabin site, the willow wand writhing in his hands. But my parents were skeptical about the efficacy of dowsing or water witching. Besides, we hadn't the money to hire a drilling rig, and hand-dug wells are an over-whelming project for a man working alone.

In the red dirt my father piled at the side of the cistern, the ant lions made their pits, I my sacrifices—ants, an occasional stunned fly. When I tired of feeding them, I could dig them up easily. Scraping up dirt and doodlebug together, I'd blow the dust out of my hand leaving the bewildered bug in my palm. Despite the ominous jaws, the larva was just that—larval, grub-pale. Then, in a half whisper I began my incantation:

Doodlebug, doodlebug! Backup, backup!
Doodlebug, doodlebug! Backup, backup!

And the doodlebug would. But this was not the magic.

Encouraged by the drone of a voice or frightened by the puffs of breath when I popped my *p*s, the bug circled backward in a closing spiral. If I cupped my palm into a creased depression, it would spin into the crack and disappear. There I sat ("Happy as if I had good sense," as my mother used to say), the jaws of the underworld en-closed in the crease of my palm, and the heavenly city spreading out around me in all directions.

The Drownt Boy

The woods are lovely, dark and deep

"Did they find that drownt boy yet?"

The man asking wears a new straw hat. His wife has rolled down the passenger-side window. I just arrived at this Forest Service campground, Akers Ferry, Missouri, last night. I've planned on a three-day canoe trip down the Current River with my stepson, Reese.

I am no help, though I am well informed. I know, for instance, that I'm about twenty-five miles from the cabin where I charmed doodlebugs thirty-some years ago. Having read up on the local dialect, I could tell the man he retains speech patterns Elizabethan or older. His forebears crossed the Atlantic speaking a country dialect archaic in Shakespeare's time. I'm thinking of the words I looked up last week, old words: cowcumber for cucumber, sparrowgrass instead of asparagus. Wrastle . . . chaw . . . bile for boil . . . declinations like ketch and kotch . . . Elizabeth's habit of dropping the terminal *g* in her writing. . . . More to the point, the shift from *t* to *d* leaves modern Americans saying salad for the original sallet, ballad for ballet, and drowned for drownt.

I hadn't known there was a drownt boy.

Last night, after we'd settled in and begun building a fire, I noticed the bottoms of the picnic tables in the campsite plastered with
leaves, though the sandy soil was dry. The tables, lashed to the fire
grills with wire, strain at the ends of their tethers. A flood within the
last week for sure. We are on our way to the park concession to rent a
canoe.

" . . . church group from Illinois," the man is saying, pronouncing
the *s* in Illinois as do many people in the South and Midwest. "They
had to pull that counselor back out. Almost lost him too. Boy told
them he could swim and wouldn't wear any jacket. I hope they find
him, for the parents' sake."

"When was the flood?" I ask after a polite silence for the dead and
the grieving.

"Friday." (It's Tuesday.) "Fourteen foot of water come across this
end of the campground."

Noting this further Elizabethanism—the plural of foot: foot; of
maple, oak, and pine: maple, oak, and pine—I pump the hat man for
more information. Is the river going to drop any further? If the rain
holds off. Is it supposed to rain? Nobody knows. Would he go in the
river? If he were younger, if he had a life jacket and somebody who
was a good hand with canoes. Reese and I leave to talk to the rangers
and the concessionaires.

On the way through the campground, we see the scouts of a pack
of Ozark hounds—escaped hunting dogs that scrounge around the
campground. They look sorry-assed, wet and bedraggled. It's too
cold and foggy to get on the river, so I dawdle, try to gather my
thoughts from yesterday's long trip down. I tell myself to be only
where I am.

When I was a difficult teenager, my mother's advice was always
"Don't harden your heart." I'm sure she meant it differently, but
right now it seems a reproach for being more concerned with form
than content. The drownt boy is not only no kin to the old man, but
one of the thousands of tourists who pass through this country every

year, tourists who mimic the locals' speech and make fun of their
dress and the signs of poverty.

The river looks uninviting, foul and cold. The longer a body stays
in the water, the more time there is for the elements and the wildlife
to work. Crawfish and eels leave their marks. And the water. Waiting
for the fog to burn off, I leave Reese to explore on his own while I talk
to rangers and watch the proprietors get the ferry working again.

Beside the ranger office at the park entrance, a johnboat is trail-
ered in. With its flat bottom and jet outboard, it can navigate as much
of the river as a canoe, jetting over rapids, riffles, submerged logs.
Searchlights attached to a handrail extend two or three feet off the
bow. Batteries wired in series cover the flat bottom. Night searches.
The jeep carries the logo of the Missouri State Underwater Recovery
Team. The diver running his equipment check has the build of a
swimmer and the bearing of a Marine. He wears a mustache, beret,
and gun. His curt nod defers all questions to the local ranger, who
probably knows the river better.

The river is open, life vests required. A tolerable canoeist should
have no problem. The higher water—two feet above flood stage—
means fewer problems in this intermediate stretch. The central channel is deeper, the boulders submerged. The worst danger is that more
rain might fall on the saturated slopes. The trip will be duller, the
water clouded with sand, the wildlife less active. I normally spot
several kinds of fish from the silent canoe—trout, bluegill, eels, perhaps a flotilla of alligator gar cruising purposefully through the blue
water at the edges of pools. Fishing is shot anyway because we have
ruined both our reels. My fault—I didn't clean and oil them before I
threw our snarl of gear in as a hedge against boredom.

I've come for research, for rest, for a contact with the closest
extensive forest to Nebraska, where I live. Fortunately, the area around
Omaha has riverine forest, eroded hills and bluffs that extend the
eastern oak-hickory range in fingers out toward the plains. Due south,
the outriders of the Ozarks nick the edge of Kansas into Oklahoma.

The ferry uses waterpower with an assist from an electric outboard. Attached to a cable hung over the river, the craft is shackled on in such a way that cranking a handwheel will orient the flat side of the pontoons at an angle to the current, causing it to tack across the stream. It nosed ten feet up the bank in the flood. The concessionaires spend an hour prying it off the bank, as I watch and put off the decision. When they get it working, they bring across another ranger, whom I dutifully ask for advice, and who carefully avoids advising me.

Getting an answer is sometimes hard here. Local folks can't say it's dangerous. I'm not going to have an easy trip any way I look at it. What can they tell me? I take pride in my lack of pride on such occasions. No need for me to prove anything by insisting on running the river. I know I'm a fair hand at handling a canoe in water like this, and that I wouldn't want to try much more of a challenge than this river offers. I know I'm a poor swimmer. I also know swimming doesn't amount to much where one never has to swim more than ten yards to the bank, but where the current can overpower the strongest swimmer who tries to fight it. Soon the search helicopter arrives for refueling—another excuse to dawdle.

The drive here, on Memorial Day weekend, brought us in late afternoon to what I describe to my noncamping Midwest friends as a baby wilderness. The river is rated "class two" for riffles, root wads, and occasional white water. You can drown in your bathtub, I remind them. All the campgrounds in the upper reaches have running water, and people camp on the gravel bars with little regard to the printed warnings, relying on the rangers to come past if a flash flood threatens.

Still, the river is not an amusement-park ride. There's no one to sue if you break your leg or drown, or lose your canoe and camping gear and die of exposure. On the way down we passed Kansas City. Off the belt highway the water towers of Gladstone, Pleasant Valley, and the other generic suburb towns rose above the foliage until we passed the scaffolding marking the rides of Worlds of Fun, with its concomitant water attractions, Oceans of Fun and Rivers of Fun. What's next, I remember thinking, Savannahs? Mountains? Ghettos and Third Worlds of fun?

Now I'm irritated. Why couldn't the Weather Service have warned me? Why can't the rangers give me better advice? Why can't I decide? A boy drowned. He was jacking around, not wearing a life jacket. People drown in swimming pools. This is not a swimming pool. What will we do for three rainy days? This will not be a nostalgic chance to recall my pastoral childhood. It's never been comfortable country.

Driving, I became absorbed in figures—partly as a way to keep Reese from being more bored than he had to be. Average miles per hour, per gallon—number of hours till lunch, the next sizable town. My private calculations were more Pythagorean. Problem: If, as Wolfe says, we can't go home, exactly how close can we get? My itinerary, dreamed up under the influence of half-understood accounts of chaos theory, superstrings, and twistors, tried to sneak in on the subject by imagining the path of a logarithmic spiral. (If you remember your basic geometry or art history, you will recognize this as the one superimposed over the dimensions of the Parthenon or the human figure to demonstrate that its ratio is the same as that of the golden rectangle—r x 1.618.) On this course, we can come infinitely close to the center, without reaching it. Lately, I have seen this as a comfort rather than a frustration.

My route along the Missouri, overshooting its sharp eastward curve in a gentler veering up into the peneplain, will take me south of Reynolds County. Named for a territorial governor and one of the most isolated and precipitous areas in the region, the county is resistant to the blunt approach. I'll circle back on it, driving at the end of the river trip down the gravel tram road, past my parents' and grandparents' former farms in the red-dirt ridge country. Nonetheless, I expect these truths in my personal hermeneutics will have changed by the time I reach them.

Milky clouds form and disappear in the water. The sand, rock flour, and forest duff aren't dissolved in the water, but, kept in motion by the current, they aren't settling out as rapidly as usual. I think of tea leaves, the drift of genes in the local breed of dogs, Brownian motion, the random drift of people and things. Unlike me and the other human constituents, these particles don't give a tinker's damn where they end up. The river itself doesn't care that around the turn of the century logging companies came, having logged out the north woods, to lay waste its shores. It is by nature a sandy river. Logging has overlaid the sandbars with a layer of gravel. What the glaciers did not do in thousands of years, humans did in less than a decade. As it was impervious to glaciation, to seas, to all but time and gravity, the river also ignored history.

Gravel or sand, we can't camp on the bars, and can't fish the pools. The water is the corpse-white of the root grubs we used to dig for catfishing. Finding them near the surface means a late frost in local lore. The one time I got finned by a catfish caught on worms and bobbers from a stock pond, it stung for days. Though we could get reels and bait at the store, the river shows no sign of clearing. Maybe just camping in this doubtful weather will keep us busy for three days. Last night was pleasant enough.

After breaking the reels on a few practice casts, we headed back to our campsite in the beginnings of the long summer dusk, cool for this time of year, few fireflies out. The calico hounds were coming closer to camp with evening, the pack a regular sampler of the local varieties. Beagle is the obvious strain, but the Ozark hound's genes haven't settled yet into a true breed. Here again, the spiral is at work, the helical DNA. The shape is more efficient at packing than any shown in my old Boy Scout handbook, whether it is packing information on the growth of cells, packing leaves on a branch to make the most efficient exposure to sunlight, or packing water molecules down a whirlpool in the river.

At work also is a kind of Brownian motion—the random groupings of strains and breeds producing this recognizable pattern with wide random variations. Tourists lose or abandon their pets, adding to standard a mix of beagle, redbone, bluetick, and such. I detected a pit bull's head on one especially personable con man of a hound who did an excellent imitation of heeling, and rubbed affectionately against my leg, scratching the scabbed remnants of an ear on my jeans. His scalp was braided with scars thick as stretch marks. He didn't turn mean when I waved him away with my rod, but cocked his head as if expecting me to throw this cumbersome stick for him to fetch.

Later, as we blew at the pile of kindling, sticks and paper that grew damper as we fanned and puffed in the thick river air, the pack of hounds came ripping through the clearing, scarface at their head. At the forest edge stood a rail-thin hound, whippet shaped, champagne colored. Its head was down, its tail tucked, and it stood at the forty-five-degree angle to the onslaught that implies submission. The pack was not merciful. Scarface butted chests with the newcomer, while three others worked the flanks and rear. When it looked as if they were going to draw blood, we chased them off with pieces of firewood. The newcomer sidled toward our campground, but kept her distance, just at the periphery of what would become the campfire's glow. We could see she was female, starved thin, and had what looked like a brand. The numerals 103 were plainly visible across her side. Outlined in pink hair, the body of the numbers appeared hairless, the skin the same color as her pale coat. She shivered convulsively. The leaves rattled in the river reeds and underbrush nearby where she finally curled up, another small spiral. Soon, she stopped shivering and began to dream. We could hear whimpers, the occasional rhythmic motion of a dog sleep-running. Chasing something, or running away?

Just before dark, a ventriloquist owl began hooting on the near slope. We swept the watercolor wall of spring foliage with my binoculars, but saw nothing. Our hearing was not directional enough to locate a likely patch of trees given the acoustical complexity of the hollow—the damp air, the natural resonance of the owl's voice, and the many surfaces: slopes, rock outcroppings, millions of leaves, and the boles of trees. The owl hooted again late—horned owl, more common than the barred owls that also roost here according to the guidebooks, though I have never seen or heard one. In the dark, shut in by campfire glow in the nearly deserted campground, memory reworked landscape. Two ridges close in on one another here, a third running between them. This is a fair-sized hollow where a major tributary, Gladden Creek, enters the river. Probably, both were flooded Friday.

After the owl, after 103 had stopped running in her sleep, after Reese had gone to bed and I'd sat stirring the embers of the campfire for a half hour, I crawled into the tent. My face was tight from the smoke and dry heat of the fire, my lips chapped. Sleep came easily, but I woke immediately. The effect of the daylong drive was telling. In a panic, close to the fear of falling, I started up, my dream of water sliding past turned into a highway. Thought I'd fallen asleep at the wheel. Years ago I spent so much time on the road, I experienced this almost every night. I'd reverse the image, turn the road into water, and play a soundtrack in my head—Mississippi John Hurt's "Slidin' Delta," sung in the deep delta accent, the hint of Cajun in the vowels ("poity baby"), accompanied by his bottleneck slide guitar:

> Oh the slidin' delto
> > run right by my baby's door.
> yes that . . . delto
> > run right by my . . . door.

The ellipses articulated by the steel strings sliding those vowels around in the same dialect.

The effect that woke me and the one that put me to sleep are the same. "The spiral aftereffect" it's properly called, the "spiral effect" for convenience. Stare at moving water—a waterfall, a fast smooth-sliding stream—at a moving conveyor belt or at the highway directly in front of your car, and then look away. The sensation of motion remains. At the turn of the century, this perceptual phenomenon was much studied but then abandoned as a research subject because the results of experiments were of "limited usefulness."

Before sleep, I remembered another old song:

> Oh, Johnny doodlebug, come up, come up.
> Come up and I'll give you
> a bushel of corn.

Now it's morning. Johnny Doodlebug, the drownt boy, the clear, still feeling of surety won't surface. The man in the car, the rangers, the canoe rental concessionaire, no one can tell me the river is safe. Hell, the river is never safe for a fool. I talk to Reese, and he promises to wear his life jacket. If it rains, we will have to leave the river. Talking about thunder draws lightning, a local belief says. I think of contraries, the holy clowns of the plains Indians—timid heroes who dreamed of lightning. It's time to go.

We pick up our canoe on a flooded gravel bar. The green Forest Service garbage cans half float, chained to posts or willow shrub. We carry food, tent, bags, and supplies for three days. I spend half an hour packing and repacking, balancing the load and tying it in with parachute cord. Things we may want quickly—rain gear, heavy shirts, a change of pants, first aid, a map—I've sealed in a five-gallon plastic bucket, the bail tied to a thwart. I tether a collapsible three-gallon water jug so we can pass it back and forth.

The man who brings the canoe says they lost seven cars from the "floater's lot," a leveled-out section of the gravel bar through which river trees—sycamores, cottonwoods—have risen in the eighty-some years since the gravel washed here. Leaving Reese with the canoe, I drive to the grassy field next to the store, about twenty feet above the river. On the way back I stop by the store to buy a river bag, strong polyethylene that rolls into a watertight seal at the top and fastens with clips. This is for wallet, car keys, extra matches, and other loose valuables. The woman at the counter is counseling another group— two couples, fifties and thirties—I take for parents, daughter, and son-in-law.

The concession is the most automated operation I've seen. We stand about with computer-printed receipts while she checks the screen to see whether any of the outlets downstream have started renting. The lower river is closed. Barring more rain, it should open in the two days it will take us to get there. Others are above us and below us on the river, though no one has checked in yet. Our downstream course is thick with rangers and volunteers looking for the drowning victim. Upstream, the floodwaters are down a bit more, but the springs are gushing, sending two-foot waves across the narrow channel. The foursome, having run that section before, decide to go upstream. I step out, jog down to the landing. Reese, not yet bored at my delay, skips rocks across the steely surface.

"Pretty Saro" is an old song from the British Isles that's harbored in the hills. "She came like the sun on the morning mist," it says, "and burnt my poor heart away." That is what's happening here. Shivering damp of moments ago is giving way to intense sunlight. I insist on sunblock for necks, upper arms, and legs, though Reese scoffs. The life jackets are too galling to stand in long, so we put out into the slack water over the flooded bar, stroke upstream to round clumps of flooded willow, and, with some jerkiness, turn into the current to begin the process of learning to function smoothly together.

We are wandering. That's what one does on the Current. The well-named river doesn't burble or splash, roar or threaten, but slides like smooth whiskey, clear and clean. Its snakelike ease tells you this is not high mountain water ready to fly back into air as mist or spray, but earthier water with more of the undertone of deciduous forest. It has a swimmer's uncoiled strength. When light falls across it, it is as if a very fine oil were floating on the surface—linseed, olive—palliating the glare and reflection like an old master's coat of varnish, or the glow of hand-rubbed wood.

In the balance between the smooth flow of the water and the impediment of cliff and boulder, this river is the oldest master. The worst obstacles are not rocks, but overhanging tree limbs. Branches of waterlogged deadheads jut out and shake with the hidden power of the current. And root wads. These upturned gorgons' heads of tree roots in the stream trap the current in a strange sibilant foam and will cage a canoe in their upturned arms. The gnarled roots are hard and sharp. They can impale a swimmer with their sharp ends, catch clothing. The undertows around them are as labyrinthine as the roots themselves. A swimmer trapped underneath must fight both.

We have probably floated within fifty feet of the corpse in our first five minutes of canoeing.

We are living flotsam, wandering. The prairie-mountain-northern-southern river slides past riffles. Curves with whirlpools on their downstream side catch at the stern where I sit, mostly steering by back paddling. Reese spends excess energy practicing prystrokes and drawstrokes in the dead stretches.

One advantage of this section of the river is its evenly spaced springs, cliffs, and caves. It will not be boring for Reese. Besides the great blue herons stroking up off the water a bend ahead of us or watching us pass from the branches of a dead tree at riverside, little wildlife shows itself. The usually ubiquitous turtles have few midstream rocks for sunning. The sun is fickle anyway. We pant in wide dead stretches steaming in sun, then tuck behind a bend as clouds come with a shivering wind at our backs. Below rock outcroppings, pools—called holes locally, and named (Baptizing Hole, Big Solution Hole)—drop forty feet. Usually, one can see white sand through ten or fifteen feet of water. Their color—normally preternatural blue, India ink dissolved in clear water—is milky now, sometimes cornflower blue where rock flour and sand mix with springwater. In one such hole we sit still while the curling current brushes up off the rocks and across the bottom of the aluminum canoe. The sand is coming back. We can hear its static, white noise hissing beneath us.

Five miles downstream, we find Cave Spring on the north side of this east-running stretch. Curves swing the southwest-running river from due north to due west. I see the hole first, still water behind a low wall of rock jutting out into the stream, a johnboat nosing out of it. Voices come from the main channel, blocked from view by a bend and overhanging branches. One of the outboards revs. A ranger in the johnboat calls to let the other know we're coming. Around the obstruction now, I see the second boat's single occupant, a large man, I'd guess 250 pounds, not a ranger, but a local helping with the search. His bow points at the sky.

"Nothing here," the ranger calls. We turn sideways in the current on the far side to take the wake of the powerboats head-on. They pull off, and we paddle into the pool.

This is the confluence of two rivers. Once we pull out of the current, we're in slack water for a few strokes. Then we're breasting the nameless underground tributary pouring from the cave before us. I tell Reese to stroke, and he does so hesitantly, asking how far we'll paddle. The cave runs only fifty yards into the bluff before it dives down. Reese is uncomfortable and starts back paddling, but breaks off to wave his paddle at swallows diving past his head. He stops when I assure him they're not bats. I remind him that the pool could be hundreds of feet deep, and we have to paddle together to maintain control.

For the first few yards, ferns and strange wildflowers grow along crevices in the rock, remnants of the flora here during the ice age, trapped in this cool sanctuary since. Then the light grows too weak for even these, and we see only rock, black with water seeps and clayey mud. Just before the light grows too feeble to see, we come to a curve and the end of the tunnel. Looking back toward the mouth, we can see the mushrooming upwell of the spring. We are floating on a fountain, suspended on a column of water. When we drift against the bank, Reese holds us against the rock of the upslanting cave floor with his paddle. He has been nervous this whole silent slide into the dark—understandably so, since he's in the front of the canoe, with little between his knees and blackness. Now, with a touch of land, he wants to get out on the slick wet rock and explore the cave. I veto that with a quick back paddle, and explain my reasons later: slick rock, the difficulty of getting in and out of the canoe in the dark with steep slopes above and below the waterline, and the fungus that grows in caves. I'm sure many people have explored this cave, but the murky water, the intermittent overcast, and the ever-present reminders of the rangers, divers, and local volunteers make me cautious. In better weather, the water glows with sunlight reflected off sand through the south-facing mouth. Canoes or sticks floating there seem suspended in air. Even today's sandy water glows slightly from beneath.

On the first curve after the cave the eggbeater rhythm of the helicopter comes at us from downstream, driving a pair of great blues. They break off above us and roost in the trees just out of sight past the green wall of foliage. The helicopter drifts in and out of sight, checking the brush on either side of the river where the floodwaters may have lodged the body. Most of the rest of the day, it is ahead of us. We passed divers early on but are now beyond their search area. If, as seems most likely, the body lodged on the bottom, it will be within a few hundred yards of the campground. If it floated further, it may be hung up in trees or brush.

Two or three times we smell carrion as we pass flat, low gravel bars covered with brush. Turkey vultures, usually seen as grand silhouettes over the cliffs, perch on snags above us. Reese asks what they are, and I tell him, but he doesn't believe me until we drift right under one perched on an overhanging snag. Now obvious is the shape of the body, the beak, the collar ruff, the septic-looking blue-black rind of the head, naked, to be thrust into dead flesh without having the corruption stick. They're doing the same thing the helicopter is, looking for the drownt boy, I think out loud.

"Very funny," Reese says in reprimand.

Not to the vultures.

Kingfishers work the river. They complain, then commiserate as the helicopter makes another pass. In wide stretches, a couple of power lines cross the river. The birds' blue bodies sway there, goofy topknots looking like a schoolboy's cowlick, as they dubiously scan the stirred-up water for a meal.

In these widenings of the channel, other creeks come in, winding across defunct fields. The Forest Service bought the few homesteads that survived logging and erosion when the riverway legislation went into effect. Here I usually hear a round of bobwhites, the call of one fading into the next until a single voice paces the canoe down the river. I try a few calls, whistling:

Bob, Bob White!

But they aren't out, though the sky is clearing and the breaking bits of cloud are bright whitecaps in a sun-drenched bay. The temperature nears eighty, still low for this time of year. I try again, a rising inflection, like a bartender, paging Bob to come to the phone:

Bob? Bob White?

Sorry, lady. If your husband's here, he's not answering.

I reach down to get my binoculars out of the case, the strap of which is looped over the crossbar of the canoe. When I realize they're not there, I remember rearranging the gear in the bucket to make room for them. It takes a bit of struggle to work the top off, but when I do, they aren't there either. I set them in the gravel next to the canoe, gravel with a fine coating of mud, about the same color as the binocular case. It could have blended in well enough that I missed it in my last scan of the bar before we left. Then again, I could have absentmindedly scooped them up with the fishing gear, traveling clothes, and the like and put them back in the trunk. For the time being, I will have to rely on my unaided eyes to spot what little wildlife is out. Soon I am able to think of it as an advantage, a chance to develop my spotting skills.

Soon we are hungry. We pull in at Pulltite campground, an agreeable park with shade trees, picnic tables, toilets, and a small concession store. The beach picnic area is fairly active. A pair of kayakers is ahead of us, and a young couple pull in after us. Both have camped on gravel bars overnight, and both downplay the danger of flood. The young couple are leaving the Current to go south for the Eleven Point River. They say a heavy rain will wake you up, and it's a simple matter to move uphill if you site your camp well. The kayakers feel the same and plan to camp on gravel bars again tonight.

I've camped on the bars only once. I had thought of gravel-bar camping tonight, but I am taking the local's word and respecting the river. Here, respect (pronounced "respet" as in the Aretha Franklin song) is important to folks. You show it to the river. You show it to others in a humble attitude that outsiders often take for simpleness. You insist on it yourself—shocking the tourists at times with a sudden gruffness when they become patronizing.

A couple of writers I met years ago innocently ran afoul of an elderly woman storekeeper in the Ozarks. Camping and fishing along the nearby White River, they'd stopped at a roadside grocery for supplies. Noticing a private trail down the steep bank, they asked if it would be all right to go bathe in the river.

"Go on down there, but you don't *wont* to get in that *river* here," the lady said with the peculiar emphasis that gives outsiders pause. Asked why, all she'd say was, "It's a thang there."

Further pressure finally got her angry. She walked up to one of the nice young city boys with her hand out, thumb and fingers touching into a peak, stuck the tip of her fingers in his face, and made a snatching gesture.

"A thang! A thang," she half whispered. "It'll git ye." And pulled the grasping mouth of her fingers down, as if underwater.

Snapping turtle? Undertow? Haint? What difference? They didn't go in.

A canoe full of equipment is a lovely thing. The camping supplies are mostly backpacking gear. The pack stove weighs under two pounds, and a fuel container with under a quart of white gas will cook our dinners with enough fuel left over to help start damp kindling. We're not riding low, unbalanced, or top-heavy. The pack frame and pail wedged under a crosspiece seem to stiffen the aluminum body. With a few pounds more food, we could travel the entire 105-mile scenic riverway. It's deceptive. Though the flooded river is easier and faster to run, there are sharp bends and esses to navigate. Fallen trees cross the glassy *V*s of deep water pointing downstream to the chutes. Normally this is where we'd want to be, so we have to confer on the second-best way.

The little green heron, or shitepoke, is out now, perched on dead branches, low to the water, neck pulled in till the head rests between the shoulders, a goiter protruding at the front. If we are still we can approach close enough to see wet feathers on the breast, parted to show the white skin beneath, the scaly legs, much more substantial than the spindly great blue's. Still no turtles, and probably few frogs— the shitepoke's patience goes unrewarded.

We pull in to explore gravel bars or to climb in shallow caves. Deeper caves have grills across their mouths—both to shield floaters from their own lack of self-control and to protect the inhabitants. Several species of bats used to inhabit the caves, but the larger gray bats are endangered now. Because they provided the guano that supplied the caves with nutrients, this is a serious loss. We are planning a cave tour tomorrow morning at Round Spring Cave. The cave, not connected to Round Spring, has its own stream flowing through it.

Approaching the campground is exciting. The river this far down either braids into several channels, runs slowly through deep pools, or rushes in rough chutes where it is pinched between cliffs. Where cliffs, therefore ridges, come together on both sides is also the logical place for a road. Just before the campground, we rush past a highway bridge. Whirlpools on either side of us knock hefty limbs against the bottom of the canoe. At one point we have to maneuver between willow stands in deceptively swift water because the main current is so fast and I am unsure whether I will recognize the landing in time.

The parking lot is three-fourths flooded. We paddle twenty yards past the boat launch, across the lot where people usually park their trucks and trailers. This section of the river is more frequented by powerboats, though few even here use exposed props because of the rapids and the frequency of submerged boulders. When we put our waterlogged feet to ground, we are near the confluence of the spring branch, which we can see flowing through the trees, also flooded. I hope the flooded woods simply mean that the rising river has backed up the spring branch, not that the spring itself is flooding. Round Spring is one of the biggest, and since these complicated large springs are relatively even in flow, it would mean that the entire drainage system is saturated. If so, the floodwaters are going to be slow to dissipate as we go downstream, and even a little rain will make the river dangerous.

The sky at the moment is gloriously clear, but that means nothing.

Setting up camp at the end of a leg-numbing day of canoeing is endorphin-producing effort. By the time we have dragged the canoe far above the waterline, taken up our last load to the well-groomed campground fifty feet above the river, set up the tent, and gathered firewood from the nearby firepits, we are ready to explore a bit.

The roof of the cave bearing Round Spring's underground river collapsed, leaving a round hole about fifty yards wide with a blue pool at the middle. The water flows back under the rock for a hundred yards and finally spills forever out of the hillside. Aboveground, this fast, deep stream flows a third of a mile to join Spring Valley Creek, thus becoming the last and by far the largest of many spring branches to empty into the creek before it, in turn, becomes a tributary of the

Current River. The spring is flooded. The water is murky and the spring branch is over its banks. On the way to the small roadside store up on the highway, we cross the spring branch on a low-water bridge. Cars are using the bridge, though a trickle of water is seeping across the top.

I have my dry shoes on after a day of soaking my feet in bilge water, so I take them off to walk across the bridge. A low-water bridge is just a raised concrete roadway with one or more culverts running through it. The two culverts here generate two long whirlpools, and on the opposite side two streams of water. Another stream jets out between concrete seams in miniature imitation of the large processes that strain and work beneath us.

In the quiet water near the downstream bank, Reese points out what look like snakes. Two brown eels glide sideways along the bridge, looking as if they are pennants run back and forth on a cord. The floodwater feels suddenly unnatural and unhealthy, even this clear brook. I've seen fish with eel bites on them—vicious, algae-ringed hickeys, through which the eel tries to suck out the fish's life. As I stand feeling the warm, dry, slightly dusty cement against my wet feet, I think of their hideous mouths and shudder. As if someone were reading my thoughts, a close, intimate sound insinuates itself behind my ear.

The whirlpools are sucking and belching air, two watery flower mouths at the ends of long stems. A squeak. A gurgle. Then a long kissing sound such as adolescent boys make against the backs of their hands to embarrass young couples. One of the whirlpools has a tangle of barkless limbs caught in its throat. Out of the gargle and susurus, there are irregular poundings as a loose log, too long to get through, rattles against the mouth of the culvert.

We cross the spring branch, pass the bloated spring, and explore as far as the entrance of the cave we will tour tomorrow. The cave spring is rushingly clear; the smaller spring branch that originally carved the rock now exits the ground further up the valley, a beautiful stream in which, from the small footbridge, I see trout, lithe existentialists dedicated only to the most immediate truths of feeding and procreating and dying. Men call them monsters, giants, grandfathers if they live a few years and grow to over a foot and a half. And they are right, for there is something old in them, a leviathan quality unrelated to their size. Here, for all that they are introduced, I welcome the flash of their bellies in this clear pool where we have all been herded by the flood. They help me forget the unclean feeling of the floodwater, the obscene suggestions of the vortex mouths, the gaseous belches of a river that could swallow thousands of drownt boys, whose tributary once sucked me under and held me down like a schoolyard bully.

Reese also helps. Despite his size, he is still boy enough not to be able to resist teasing me. Crumbly, six-foot-tall stalks of last year's dead milkweed or nettle stand next to the walkway. Reese designates these "woogie sticks," which means he picks them and follows behind me, poking at my ears yelling "Woogie-woogie." Asinine. Childish. Annoying. I grab one and drop into as much of a fencing stance as I can remember from the course I took fifteen years ago to chase him across the footbridge.

There has been a skunk in our campground within the past day, and another pack of dogs is about. We hear them barking but never see them. While we are trying to get the wet wood burning, I hear them coming through the thick underbrush surrounding our campground. The area supports a surprising variety of ground cover, from dry, piney ridges to the lush, semitropical hollows and river margins. Here, we are on the western edge of a finger of southern pine forest that runs up parallel with the Mississippi. Suddenly, the hounds are right behind me, snarling, fighting a stranger, or a skunk. I turn at bay, a piece of firewood in my hand. Reese is safe, down at the bathroom washing smoke out of his eyes. It's too wet and cold for skunks or dogs to have rabies. The most immediate danger is skunk spray.

No skunk. No dog, or raccoon. I stand foolishly threatening a dense wall of shrubs—chinquapin saplings, sassafras, sumac—woven together with strands of poison ivy. I have been warning Reese about poison ivy all day, and I nearly backed into it. I usually succumb to small, unexpected dangers, I remind myself. The heel blister filling my boot with blood; forgetting a can opener and trying to open a can with an ax; slicing my thumb while cutting apple pieces to entice my daughter down a trail. When the adrenaline stops pumping, I realize that the moist evening air carries sounds, and must have made the dogs seem much closer than they were.

By the time we have the fire burning, we are almost too tired to enjoy it. We warm ourselves well, and I sit up after Reese has turned in, walking down to the river once to check the canoes and look at the sky (no stars visible to the west where the weather's been coming from) before I bank the fire and crawl into the tent. Tonight it is rushing water rather than highway that appears when I close my eyes. I try to decide why I prefer the water imagery. Romanticism? Spilt religion?

Is that thunder I hear? A car starting up? There is no light. It is 2:00 A.M.

Water

If there is magic on this planet, it is contained in water. Its least stir even, as now in a rain pond on a flat roof opposite my office, is enough to bring me searching to the window. A wind ripple may be translating itself into life. I have a constant feeling that sometime I may witness that momentous miracle on a city roof, see life veritably and suddenly boiling out of a heap of rusted pipes and old television aerials. I marvel at how suddenly a water beetle has come and is submarining there in a spatter of green algae. Thin vapors, rust, wet tar and sun are an alembic remarkably like the mind; they throw off odorous shadows that threaten to take real shape when no one is looking.

Loren Eiseley, "The Flow of the River,"
from *The Immense Journey*

THE TRICK IS TO BE LOOKING AT THE RIGHT TIME. Some trick—watch the moving pool too long and the spiral effect dulls your vision. But look away and you may miss the moment. Of course, someone always is looking—tree, water beetle, algae—and keeping record. About the time Eiseley was writing this, I was keeping lookout around the cistern for doodlebugs, watching the woodland pond at the bottom of our draw for pollywogs. Rafts of frog eggs hung around a flat rock that offered better access to the water than the muddy banks. They were balls of jelly, clumped together, organs, eyes with thousands of slit irises staring. I pulled them out to dry.

Despite parental warnings, young boys are drawn to water. Ponds, creeks, and wells are the street corners where a country boy can hang out and learn about life. My mother warned me away from the cistern, and would have been horrified to imagine me creeping over the old boards to peek down the well beside my grandparents' house. I had heard one could see stars reflected in the water, but all I saw were the stone sides of the hand-dug hole, graying off into darkness.

Down in that darkness lies most of the water in the Ozarks. Not satisfied with having sculpted the surface of the land, water honeycombs the limestone underneath it. By freezing and thawing the upper soil layers, it covers cleared fields and even the bare spots under the pine trees with chert. I also looked, with my father's help, down an abandoned well at a dime of water, nothing but sky on its face. When the cistern went dry, we used the well a quarter mile from our house—at an old home site on the Vales' property. Both sources needed either boiling or purification tablets. We let the clay settle out of the cistern water before adding chlorine. The well water was clear but brackish, probably a trapped layer of local water seeping down from above, rather than a true route to the underground rivers.

The abandoned well was one of many signs of former inhabitants. Like the slate tablets my father's generation used, the land's erasures were never absolute. An abandoned orchard stood a half mile north of the Vales' well. I often dug up artifacts in our own yard—pieces of cast iron from an original settler's stove, tableware. Once I unearthed a butcher knife and practiced throwing it at tree trunks, sticking it in the ground.

My father built me a swing for my birthday, hung with brand-new rope from a blackjack oak. I enjoyed it for only part of an afternoon before my brother, five years younger, woke from his nap and de-

manded equal time. He went to tell my parents, and I remember his
look of triumph, running back across the spring grass to tell me my
mother said I had to share. Something old and buried inside me
surfaced then—sharp flint? patent medicine bottle? I don't remember throwing the knife but how it sailed through the air in its high,
slow, tumbling arc.

Dave froze. Time became like leaf shadows on the gray-white dust
of the path. I must have been eight. I called to him to move. I
thought of my parents, running down this path perhaps two years
before, clothes and some sandwiches bobbing in a pillowcase tied to
the end of a staff. They were leaving home. I had threatened to run
away, and they reasonably concluded I would be better off at home,
so they would leave. As they packed, deliberately as the knife twirling
through the May sunshine, they talked about what they would do
when they were free. I don't think they actually sang "Free at Last."
They did skip, hand in hand, down the path, through the gate, and
down the access road through the woods, almost out of sight before I
started screaming for them to come home.

Maybe I screamed; Dave didn't. He didn't move until the knife
stuck quivering in the ground perhaps a foot from him. Then he
unfroze, turned, and ran howling for the house. I got the most
memorable spanking of my life, over my father's knee, staring into the
dirt, him sitting on the new swing. The flesh grows warm. The legs
begin an involuntary jerking. Some motherload of guilt keeps you
from wanting to ask for mercy, but pride, remorse, and terror are not
enough to keep the words choked down. You will never do it again.
You will never do anything like it again. My father was silent. Even
my brother was subdued as, later, I lay across my swing, contemplat-
ing my fate in the wash of light across the ground.

The shadows from the still bright green oak leaves of spring cast
watery movements of light and shade. They ran away from each
other, then together into a center that moved somewhere else when I
looked at it. The reverse of Dante's, Hubble's, or Black Elk's expand-

ing universe with the observer at the center, this formed a dizzying vortex with no center. Think Sartre.

Water and trees, water and light. If the trees of the Courtois Hills section of the Ozarks where we lived were second growth, the underground artifacts said, so were we. Trees pulled water out of the ground, drew maps of waterways in the air. And water, on its way down to the labyrinthine channels underground, sometimes froze and pulled up pieces of history with the chert. Older settlers, the Mound Builders, the Osage and Shawnee, had left their mark as well. Along the banks of Logan Creek, miles from the county road, lay the abandoned Stall homestead in Stall hollow where we went to pick fruit in their untended and decaying orchard. We went with permission from old Bill Woodman. Confined to a wheelchair, he had to leave the house after his sister and sister-in-law died. His library came to us because there was no room at the Ziggasses, neighbors who took him in. My mother had helped the Stall women care for Bill when she was younger.

We did not have permission from the warlike Osage to search for arrowheads along Logan Creek. The site we often searched seemed to be the arrowhead factory. Many chips were obvious failures, ones that had split in half in some penultimate stage of knapping. The flint was not smooth as obsidian, and there were many mishaps, though many we found would have satisfied less discerning craftsmen. Though I felt the presence of the tribesmen there, as if they'd appear to continue the work we seemed to have disturbed, there were no Indians. If there were, they were long assimilated. Many people, including one of my uncles, claimed Indian ancestry.

There had been, I believe, few conflicts between local Indians and whites. The early French settlers cultivated the Indians, however patronizingly. By the 1800s, refugees from overcrowded Kentucky and Tennessee were more comfortable among the few remaining tribespeople than among their newly civilized compatriots. The Osage claimed all the Ozarks before the whites got there, but the Courtois Hills were used only as hunting land. The main Osage conflicts were further west. The Shawnee stayed awhile to escape persecution to the east, and the Cherokee crossed the area on one of their trails of tears. There was good hunting, and the woodsman wants only a patch of corn and some greens around the cabin site. With better farmlands in the West, the sea of expansion flowed around the strange islands of uplands. Even the inlets of tillable river bottom and the central plateau tempted few. I am always surprised to think that the bloodiest battles of the wars of expansion happened at places like Little Big Horn, Wounded Knee, or the Alamo. Undoubtedly, I'm looking with jaundiced eyes, but the forests of the Ozarks seem a pleasanter piece of dirt to fight over than any stretch of plains. Perhaps I'm not thinking like a mounted horseman.

So events flowed past the Ozarks. The underground water stayed, gift of the humid riverlands on two sides, stored rainwater held in the limestone of the slight uplift. Even when dry years parched the western plains, the circulatory system kept pumping. Dry ridges, and wet river bottoms. From hillside to creek bottom, water and chert mark one another's course. The pinkish flint that sifts the water down through its millions of chips and keeps the steep hillsides dry also lines the bottoms of the creekbeds. Carried down through gullies and road cuts, or dug out of hillsides, they are strewn along like wood chips. Loosened from their beds, the chips seem light, and their flat edges plane them through the flood.

One derivation of the word *Missouri* traces it back to a corruption of the Siouan word for "smoky water." It applied to people who lived at the mouths of rivers, and to the drowned. Ozark water has a smoky tinge. Perhaps once the Missouri itself was closer to this hue. Seen over the red-rock bottoms in rapids, the water looks crystal. It is the clearest free-running water you'll find within two days' flat-out freeway driving. In the deep, spring-fed pools it takes on a range of indigos and milky limestone-infused blues. It is as if thousands of indigo buntings had rinsed themselves in the waters of the springs. This was the color of water mixed with the laundry bluing my mother used. She let it settle before heating it over a wood fire and pouring it into the washing machine. (A Wards model, I think, a gas-powered wringer machine with a kick starter like a motorcycle.)

I became a chip in the flood once in Logan Creek. The water was not deep blue. It was in a race, shallow enough to be swift, yet deep and straight enough to tumble me end over end. In these courses, the water takes on the milky or smoky tinge of the old name. In still pools not deep enough to be called "holes," the water is smoky green around water lilies and against granite outcroppings.

My parents were swimming in one such green pool. I remember the stillness of the water, the oak and willow boughs bending over the surface, touching it until reflection and tree fused. They swam out into the center of the pool, using the awkward crawl stroke of people who seldom swim. My father and another man, a friend who'd come with, counted how many strokes the other could take without drawing breath. They counted out loud. I remember the man splashing my mother, my father telling him to stop, an awkward moment between adults.

I stood at the foot of the pool, where it emptied into the race. Then I was head down, the pale pink stones of the bottom flowing past my head like low clouds in a mirror sky. I called out, swallowed water. The adults were running. I could see them above and below the water, their feet disconnected, their legs upside down, running over my head—me making another revolution in the current.

I was baptized in a local river, in a pool off a sandy bank. I remember the wash of water over my head, the only other time I submerged for many years. In this second baptism, there was a larger audience, and other participants, making it more official for the human community. I remember a woman who, when offered a safety pin for her skirt (we went in our Sunday best), told my aunt, "Oh, it's okay Barbry-Ruth, I'm wearing panties."

The first baptism made a more lasting impression. The land always stakes prior claim. At graduate school, I lined up on the beautiful

University of Montana oval with hundreds of students to march in our various regalia into the field house. A professor on one of those old balloon-tired bicycles with a spring-loaded front shock system rode up and down the line, getting us into formation under the lines of elms. Overhead, sparrows and evening grosbeaks fought for samaras. As we began marching, an emissary from among the boughs anointed the brown velvet trim of my hood with a squirt of white bird shit.

Seen from within the caves, the trickling underground streams look clear. The water appears antiseptic, but watch long enough and movement shows you the blind salamanders, colorlessly off-white as the rock, feeding on whatever other life subsists in the constantly fifty-four-degree water.

When I tried to drink from the roiling creek that runs the few hundred yards from Round Spring to the Current River, my father made me find the drinking fountain. Many early settlers had gotten sick and died on springwater before they'd discovered which was safe. Like wells, the springs are predictable only in their temperature, summer or winter. The hills are full of deposits of lead, zinc, and other minerals as well as ancient mounds of bat guano. Nowadays, forest service tour guides lead you through the caves. ("Bat Gwayno" one of them called it, revealing her origins as St. Louisan, where people wear "sharts" and "shart-sleeved shirts" in the summer.) A recent improvement at Round Springs is a map showing how the water in the spring arrives there. Several sources are on the other sides of ridges. Others flow deep underground, crossing under creeks and rivers to arrive at the site. If water gets turned around, it is even easier for people to lose their way.

This is small comfort to folks lost in the woods, even if those woods are familiar, even if, in the larger census of vanishing forest, the Ozark woods are not much more than the "baby wilderness" I call them. The land resists progress, and, in this resistance, there are many ways of getting lost. Following waterways, the old trick of orienteerists, isn't easy work when they all but disappear into shut-ins. Even locals end up walking miles out of their way. People were cautious about taking their bearings. Shy on matters of propriety and correctness, folks depended upon bedrock principles—unstated and labyrinthine as those underground currents that yielded only to the most skilled water witching—to see them through.

A circle a mile wide would have encompassed our cabin, the Vales' house, the farm of my Grandparents Homer, and the site where my mother's family, the Cooks, had lived in the forties. The thick forest and furrowed land made the distance seem longer—especially since, having no car, we walked everywhere.

On the way to the isolated Stall homestead, we passed my maternal grandparents' old place, in ruin by the time I saw it. The two-story log house was missing the roof to wind or to scavengers. Such salvage is not bad manners in the woods. An abandoned homestead going to rot is at least as good a source of logs—if you have the horse or mule power to haul them—as cutting down new timber and curing it.

My father's folks' place was to fall victim to both fire and salvage years later. Looking for it after an absence of twenty-five years, I almost missed it. It is easy to find, being "right up on the road" (even if that road is unknown to people twenty miles away). I didn't know the house had burned as many do here. The hand-laid stone foundation and chimney were half overgrown, some hundred yards back among the trees. (Well, that's "right up on the road" by some standards.) When I noticed my Grandmother Homer's french doors turned on their sides and used as picture windows gracing a tar-paper shack, I drove back.

Some young people swam in the reddish-brown stock pond we had never used for fear of leeches. I didn't stop. I'd lost track of my Missouri relatives. Even if my aunt and uncle still owned the property, these might not be relatives or renters at all but squatters. According to friends of my mother, many local folks have left places empty and returned to be shot at. If I introduced myself as a relative of the owners, I'd want the sheriff with me.

Though I have perhaps been gone too long to say what qualifies as Ozark standards, this is stretching hospitality. When I was a child, hunters lost in our woods would come to the cabin to ask directions and my mother would chew them out for hunting close to where children were playing. The occasional whine of a bullet and bay of hounds was part of living with open range. Armed squatters were not. They would have found a very different reception in the fifties, as would the unknown entrepreneur who stripped several miles of copper wire off the power lines.

The ruins of my mother's parents' place were out-of-bounds for me, a perfect fort with its second floor open to the sky, window casings as rifle ports. I'd sneak there often. Now a father, a grandfather, a stepfather, a teacher . . . I wonder how much of a parent's and child's knowledge of one another is based on lies—deliberate lies and those we tell despite our best efforts, lies we tell ourselves and those in which we collaborate. I swept my perimeter, sumac and sassafras advancing on the cleared yard. All clear. I inched toward the gray rotting timbers covering the well, heaved dirt clods and pieces of sandstone over it. Finding no courage to walk on it, I sat and wondered whether the water in the bottom was deep enough to drown in, or whether one sank in mud, or broke against bedrock. I once held a springy willow or alder witching stick, but it didn't point out anything. A boy's a water sprout. Obscure forces yank back and forth at him. The road past the ruined homestead to the Stall place was one tug, the memory of how my folks and I got lost taking a shortcut home another.

One full-moon night, my parents and I stayed late picking berries or fruit at the old homestead. I tagged behind them as they set off cross-country, excited and frightened by the doubt in their voices. I can't remember who was for the shortcut, who cautious. The wolves, mountain lions, and bears that by then only inhabited the deep woods of my imagination were less frightening than the full-scale argument brewing. I cleverly distracted my folks by acting tired and whining.

Both of my parents had grown up in the area, wandered the woods and farms as children, adolescents, and adults. We were in an area of a few hundred acres—smaller than some city parks. The fall moon rose among the partially bare branches; the leaves were slick underfoot. There was enough light coming through the diminished canopy to see the boles of trees clearly, but it was dark enough to hide the occasional upreaching root. Dark enough for the foxfire fungus and jack-o'-lantern glow to show through the woods. First my father then my mother recognized landmarks that put us far to the side of our intended course. Then the other argued we had walked so long, we must certainly have bypassed the house.

After revisiting the area, I begin to understand how we ended up walking in the dark long after the shortcut should have brought us home. The guidebooks give the elevation of Taum Sauk peak at 1,772 feet above sea level, lower, I believe, than the lowest elevation in several Rocky Mountain states. This is about eleven hundred feet above the lowest river bottoms, still hardly imposing. The fractal riverine valleys and the steep, eroded slopes over bases of limestone and crystalline rock make for rough walking. Though our ridgeland lay within a mile of the hollow and no more than three hundred feet higher, it was a different zone with different soil, drier climate, and different vegetation. The land is convoluted as frost, with each change of scale hiding new complications of angle and plane. The Ozarks are precisely the right scale to fool a man. Or to hide one.

The effects of erosion are severe. Caves underground, hollows above. If it has left all the land other than a couple of river valleys poor for farming, it provided many springs for thirsty woodsmen. Those that proved out were dammed and the water channeled to holding tanks and springhouses that could keep hand-churned butter cool throughout the steamiest summer. Early settlers built their springhouses to withstand bears, but raccoons have been the more enduring foe. The only functioning springhouse I saw as a child was on a bottomland farm my parents were thinking of buying. Dug into a hill, it had survived mainly as a tornado shelter. It was cooled by water running through pipes, a modern version. Though our property lacked spring or well, we were thoroughly modern with a propane refrigerator and, after the electricity came, a freezer.

The Stall place had access to water and a little triangle of bottom-land. Not the land, but the people gave out. The old maid and the widow with a crippled brother had no one to take over. Also, the road became more important than the river for transportation. The road built upon the abandoned logging-train spur followed the ridge, perpendicular to the route of turkeys, deer, turtles, bear, Indians, or woodsmen. The road is still a good place to start game, because all the game trails cross it.

Stagnation is a danger in human or hydrological terms. Only deep underground can an aquifer store the fossil water of the Great Plains' center pivot wells away from all taint of life and light. The hill culture that preserved so much of its archaic merit hidden away became less robust under the allure of the road, the telephone line, the radio wave. For most, it was money, work in the cities as throughout the rural South. The culture based on barter, subsistence farming, hunting, and local crafts became isolated, stagnant, the pockets increasingly separated. The old stories of interbreeding toward idiocy may have been literal in some places, but they are more meaningful as a symbol for what happened. Like the last grunt of the wild bears or the last mountain-lion scream, messages translated into radio beams in Nashville were yanked from the soil. As William Stafford says in his moving poem to "Ishi, the Last Wild Indian" in northern California, this process of isolation goes on until, at last, *the messages all go one way from the world.*

Folks in the hills spent most of their time alone but for the company of their immediate families. This made any civic institutions very important. Corridon consisted of a general store, a church, and three houses. The two-room school was down the road. My best memories are of the store, though the church and school were more prominent in our lives. Grogan's General Store. I have a picture of what's left, and I don't see how it could have stretched so high that harnesses disappeared into the shadows among the beams. Oiled floor. Wood stove. Smell of stove black, of bluing for guns and sheets, of dry goods and flour in sacks with print for use as shirt cloth. Sody pop in water cooler. Dog. Gas pump. Hitching post. My father and I walked there, three miles. Others drove. Or rode in.

There is a breed of horse called the Ozark trotter—sometimes fox trotter for its gait. A mixture, they have some quarterhorse, some Arabian, and some strain of paint. They vary widely in marking. Saddle horses, solid bottomed enough to plow, drag logs, or, more commonly, pull a high-sided farm wagon, they are prized for endurance and a ground-eating walk. They are good trail horses. Though the horse books don't mention it, they are quiet in the woods. I walked out the door behind my laundry-laden mother one midmorning and ran into the back of her legs as she drew up. She gasped and I peeked around her skirts. A man on a horse stood in front of our door, inside our fenced-off yard. Our dog slept.

People said no one ever saw him get off the horse. Fine by me. Furtive and isolate, he always had business, a lost cow, a runaway dog. He always came when my father was gone, asking for a glass of water, ma'am. One wanted him to leave, to stay on his horse. Bringing him a glass of water was a small price for keeping him in the saddle. Oddly bloodless, he was said to live "way back." Oh, you saw so-and-so, people would say. Did you see him coming?

I'm not sure whether this is an example of the effects of isolation on a single man or upon a young mother. Maybe he was entirely admirable, a person so in tune with his surroundings, he simply traveled quietly out of habit, out of respect. The horse was remarkable; trained and bred for the local conditions, it would stand still as the stumps in our yard. Yet, to a woman and child alone, the mounted horseman at the door is a palpable threat—as surely in the Ozarks as on the steppes of Mongolia. The Aztecs, besides having no resistance to European diseases, couldn't have known what the arrival of the caballeros meant to them and to the continent, but they were right about one thing. Mounted men are a different sort of creature. Able to carry warfare to a level exceeded only by warships, eating more grain than they were worth in useful work, these new double creatures were certainly fearsome.

Still, who can hate the pretty things? Horses evolved to run away from trouble, and it's still a trap. People continue to be suckers for them. The Spaniards caught the disease from the Moorish invasion, and passed it on to the poor forest-dwelling Indians, who left their pedestrian ways, headed out to the plains, and accommodated their entire culture to it. The cowboy is as much a slave, or what's left of him, overgrazing the land so he can ride a horse that needs a trailer and pickup truck to get it to the next overgrazed pasture. The common cold is the horse's gift to humans. The Ozarks, too marginal for extensive horse culture, relied much more on mules and developed a breed of horse that is—by horse standards—a practical beast.

If individuals were isolate and furtive, some social institutions were overt and aggressive. Pentecostalism was big. Although we belonged to a mild-mannered congregational church where my Grandpa Homer sometimes relieved the preacher and my mother played piano, you could tell that many members were used to a freer rhythm to the hymns than my mother—or the tempo notation in the hymnal— thought proper. My family and the preacher conspired to bring a guest preacher in from the NAACP.

We weren't bombed. We weren't burned. We weren't shunned. Perhaps fearing trouble, everybody forgot to come. The preacher, my parents and grandparents, and their respective families heard a stirring sermon on, as I recall, spiritual cleanliness and went back to my grandparents' for Sunday dinner. Maimie Faulkner, one of about four inhabitants of Corridon proper, also attended, because she hadn't missed in her entire life. Maimie always sang the bass parts of the hymns in a froggy voice gloomy as three days of rainy weather:

I will cling to the old rugged cross

rugged croooss

and exchange it one day for a

day for a crownnn

You may have guessed from this that we were only second-generation locals. My aunts had married in, and we were accepted. The hill folks were not as insular as at other places. My grandfather was a blacksmith from England, my grandmother a New England nanny, sent to the area for her TB (she lived into her dour eighties) and hired to look after my grandfather's children after his first wife died. My mother was born in California. It was undoubtedly from one of these foreign places they picked up their outlandish ideas. People pretended the visiting preacher incident never happened. If people were standoffish, one could hardly tell if it was because of the black preacher, because our family was "not from those parts," or because of my father's illness—which frightened people.

If water gets lost, people get lost. If water stagnates, people can too. Drink brackish water, keep cows on the thin grass of the ridges, drink their milk, and you'll get bad teeth. My dad had bad teeth, the few he had left. This wasn't his disease. His disease was epilepsy. Small wonder people were frightened; supposed sophisticates react little better. Read Dostoyevsky if you don't believe me. People felt it was what they called "a judgment from God." "An Affliction," they'd say.

There were many diseases and religions trickling into the groundwater. Money was one—also fear, xenophobia, restlessness. . . . Isolation lowers resistance.

The Drownt Boy

But I have promises to keep

Cave Tours:
Wed–Thurs: 10:00 A.M.
Fri–Sat: 10:00 A.M., 1:00 P.M.

IT'S BEEN FIVE OR SIX YEARS SINCE I'VE BEEN ON THE TOUR.
The parking lot we're standing in could hold a hundred cars. The
place ran for years as a commercial attraction before it became a
public park. Then the Park Service promoted tours heavily. Now, a
sign notes that cave tours are limited to ten people to protect the
cave's fragile interior. In this, the cave is emblematic of the region.
Isolation lowers resistance. The parking lot is empty.

We walked under the bridge on the way down. A woodchuck rolled
off a boulder and scrambled across riprap. Refusing to hurry, it stayed
carefully out of rock-throwing range. Reese hadn't seen him, so I
sailed a few pieces of flat slatey gravel beyond him and got him to
change course and come out in the open. Near the road, lazy rabbits
graze in the morning sunlight to make up for time lost to rain.

Rabbits, chucks, deer, ptarmigan—prey species constantly impress me with their lack of concern about predators. There is no mad scramble to escape upon sighting fox or cat. The only time they seem desperate is when they are hungry. Then it is sometimes hard to start them. After a first hard freeze, or in early spring, it is almost possible to step on their tails before they scramble for trees—not far up. In their watchful eyes one sees the crude beginnings of a gambler's gaze. Rabbits glance skyward while feeding ever further from cover, gauging the odds of being picked off by a circling hawk against the urgency of putting away enough food. On the other hand, I've seen so few predators in all my time in the forest, I remember even the faintest signs of them: roseate prints of cougar in the Oregon Cascades; coyote prints raying out from a well-licked bloodstain and a fluff of rabbit hair on a frozen Montana lake.

A middle-aged couple walk the trail, but they do not want the tour, only to take a picture of a real ranger. The ranger, a tall woman from New Jersey, has to go back to her truck to get her hat for the picture. She's out of uniform without it, she explains, but it's awkward in the narrow cave passages. A young couple arrive hurriedly, and we get our lanterns for the tour.

Crouching through the thirty or so yards of the low, narrow fissure forming the entryway, I realize it is more than eight years since I came here with my daughter. Willow was younger than Reese. I spend a moment envying parents who can remember their children's childhood without guilt—without collapsing holiday visits, phone conversations, and letters into an approximation of their child's adolescence. Last summer, Willow presented me with my granddaughter. I wonder what she thinks of me, my weakness for words, my inability to say what she needs to hear.

The guide takes responsibility for all of us, leaving me alone with my thoughts, humbled. I'm out of patience with myself for my Thoreauvian smugness, for thinking like Whitman that "I could turn and live with the animals," though it is true, as he says, they are "placid and self-contain'd." Neither Thoreau nor Whitman had children. I hear their words in the darkness, watch the trickle of the cave stream. What was once a rushing conduit lies open, a cave, decaying and slowly filling in over millions of years. I'm looking for blind sala-manders. A whoop up ahead, a flutter in the lights, and I put my hands up, though we have been warned against it. We confuse the tiny brown bat with our lights and movement. I force my hands down and point my face and lantern at the cave floor. Whitman would find the bats free of "the mania for owning things," and they "do not make me sick discussing their duty to God."

When Willow took the tour, the guide tricked her into smelling a pinch of ancient bat guano without telling her what it was. This guide is less aggressive. The cave tour has been shortened by almost half to protect certain chambers from the damage of human skin oil, body heat, noise, soil compaction. The odds on life are what? Six to five against?

Soda straws, stalactites and stalagmites growing together toward union in a drapery. A million years of growth could be deformed by the oil from a human hand. The tour is an exercise in slowing down time. Even a boy becomes contemplative. Things ferment slowly and more slowly as one walks away from the cave mouth where the tem-poral matters. The large Indiana bats have left the deep recesses of this cave. Species of salamanders have survived the hundreds of thou-sands of years it takes them to split into separate races on the food chain supported by the twenty-foot pile of bat droppings. Now the food flow is stopped. The cave fasts, living on reserves, a short thou-sand years' worth, say.

In a large cavern called the tobacco barn for the shape of the stalactites, the guide invites us to turn off our lanterns. We hear the slow dripping of the water, slightly acidic from steeping in leaves above. We smell the insinuation of the wine-cellar scent of cave fungi (a harmless variety in these well-visited chambers). After our eyes adjust, the afterglow of our fluorescent lanterns becomes visible, and we turn them facing the floor. The guide lights a candle in a coffee can to show the level of light available to the first explorers of caves in the area.

A few steps above the main trail, in a sort of mini-chamber set off by a curtain of grown-together drapery, is a mud puddle. Not a very large one. If you saw it in your alleyway or gravel drive one summer morning, you'd expect it to evaporate by midafternoon. It has been here for at least a million years. It is an emblem of the cave, as the cave is an emblem of the Ozarks. The species of blind salamander that inhabits this cave breeds here.

It is three to five feet in diameter, maybe an inch deep. There are tracks in the muddy sediment of rock flour where salamanders and other species have crawled. Reese notices a white "bug" in one end, a cave crawfish. Adapted to the conditions here, it moves micrometers per hour, eats slowly in the nutrient-poor waters, conserves heat. (The water and rock are constantly fifty-four degrees—the average annual outside temperature over thousands of years.) While a crawfish in the Current River lives perhaps three years, this one could be a hundred. An emblem of the Ozarks because it is delicate and hidden. Because it endures despite its fragility, outlasting hardier examples of its kind. It partakes of widely gleaned influences, yet remains itself. Because it is humble.

The passageways circle back on one another. On our exit path, the claw marks of extinct cave bears scar the solidified mud wall above our heads, made when the cave floor was higher. The bones of later residents, black bears, lay years before discovery in hollows these bears made—now off the tour. Black bears are gone too, but are being reintroduced in the southern Ozarks. Raccoons still wander in to fish for crawdads. Their prints will mark the pool edges for thousands of years.

I want to see salamanders in the stream. The young in the pool were little more than specks. Already I have forgotten whether the guide said they were born with eyes and lost them, were born with rudimentary eyes, or spent time outside before coming back and abandoning sight. The others are a bend or two ahead in the narrow passageway to the entrance. Grating bridges the narrow stream. I hold my lantern over it and peer through, check under the overhangs where the water has cut back into the rock wall. Near the entrance, I find Reese waiting for me. The others are out and the guide is waiting to lock the gate. Still no salamanders. Just before we get to the twilight caverns where some light peeps around the last curve, Reese gets to do some guiding too. He shows me a grotto where fine horsetail brush grows from a delicate stalk, white in our lantern light. We cannot tell how tall it is because it grows from behind a rock lip. A fungal growth sprouted on pack-rat dung, Reese tells me, enjoying his chance to surprise me. In a corner of the turd fungus grotto, a nematode worm is spinning an almost invisible warp of parallel silk strands.

Outside it is overcast. A box turtle that was crossing the drive to the cave parking lot has reached the berm on the opposite side and scurries into the weeds of the flooded ditch as we approach on our way back. A squirrel falls from a limb, catches itself on a lower one.

We pack the canoe and are sitting in it when the rain starts, a drizzle that becomes a shower. We move under the trees. The damp air condenses inside our raincoats. I decide against canoeing farther downstream into deeper floodwaters in what looks like a day of rain. Walking to the pay phone at the ranger's cabin, I get a ride in the back of a brand new pickup. The driver's a young man visiting the campground with his wife and young son. At the ranger station, he gets out. The rain slacks off and I reconsider yet again.

"My brother-in-law runs Akers Ferry. Tell him to come get you. Don't go down that damn river today." He gets in the truck and drives off. Fifteen minutes after I return to the canoe, the driver comes, a hired man, not the owner. His look is short of reproach. The sun is bright and steam is rising off the river into a sky without cloud.

Yesterday's trip takes fifteen minutes to retrace on the ridge roads, giving us sweeping vistas of the valley. Back at the office, I agree to wait till tomorrow (Thursday, our last planned day on the river) to settle up, perhaps run the upper reaches in a day trip. When we get in the car to drive to Eminence, a few miles past the Round Spring campground, it is nearly one o'clock.

Today, as every time I visit the famed Eminence drugstore fountain, the woman who knows how to make banana splits is out. Two doors down, the café is full of local jokes. The punch line is always "you should have seen that old boy's face." Reese says it's a town of grandpas with no grandkids. Old men populate benches outside the garage, sip café coffee, and slip out on trifling errands. On the street, a young man wearing a T-shirt from the sheltered workshop smiles and waves, and later comes into the café. Deaf, he makes himself understood in thick English and pantomime.

The young man struggles to make himself understood, and people struggle to understand. I have become accustomed to the deaf avoiding conversation with the hearing, preferring sign language as their native tongue. In isolated communities, people are either less sensitive or more honest in dealing with handicapped people. The deaf boy, the crippled girl, or the slow child is named without elaborate euphemism—"the specially challenged," or what-have-you—euphemisms ultimately insulting in their very attempts to soft-pedal their meaning.

When we return to the drugstore, the wife is still out. We get sundaes on the recommendation of a man who says he's had one every day of his life since he was sixteen. He looks about forty, six foot one or two, close to three hundred hard-packed pounds—the second heavyweight I've seen here where the body type usually runs from rangy to stringy. On the glass counter across from the fountain locally published booklets tell how to talk Ozark. The phonetics are good, if a little exaggerated. There's no mention of Pepys or Elizabeth, and nothing on the rhythm, the Ozarker's unique placement of emphasis in the sentence. I decide against ordering a real phosphate to go with my sundae.

I'm still trying to weigh the huge platters of food, an honest and vigorous language, against the tolerance, cultural events, and solvency my urban friends and I enjoy. And medical care. When I lived here in the fifties, my school bus carried us daily past the house of a man with cancer. He sat on his porch month after month, minus now an arm, now a leg, until he was a propped-up torso. His house sat so near the road, dust from passing automobiles settled on him. He'd call his wife to wipe his face and give him a drink of water. We sweated out minor illnesses—earaches, a blotchy outbreak that kept me in bed for a couple of weeks and left me shaky and sensitive to light. In which column would I place that?

On the way out of town, I try to decide whether it will be too hard on the car to detour six miles down the logging road to Jerktail Landing. I'd planned to pull out there and camp tonight. When we crest a rise, I see a car stopped in the road. An arm snakes out and points into a small roadside clearing where two tom turkeys are doing a full-fan side shuffle. One flies into the woods downhill, so the other, obeying some territorial etiquette, must fly up and across the road in the opposite direction. Tall trees, a half-acre marsh, and a steep hillside bar his way. He fights for altitude. We enjoy a display of muscle-bound flight as he spirals up to clear the trees and sinks in the dead air over the water for the hillside brush. The other tom has long since disappeared in the long, low glide more common to turkeys.

I choose the awkward course and visit Jerktail. It is the most remote campground, really not much more than a gravel bar with rudimentary facilities and easy egress in case of flood. I like camping here because no town lights, roads, or farms intrude in the narrow hollow surrounding it. A cliff across the river echoes whippoorwill diphthongs in summer dusk. Later, owls huff, tree frogs jangle, or a storm in the next county telegraphs its punches through the rock and up a camper's spine. Far enough away from the background noise, the body becomes a single sense organ.

Rain begins again as we navigate a rocky ford where the road crosses a gully. I tell Reese it's an adventure. As we arrive, a couple have just finished fishing, picnic basket and tackle on the hood of their 1968 sedan. Several floods larger than the recent one have obliterated half the riverside trees since my last trip. The downstream stretch of the campground lies on top of solid rock where the river has cut through a spur from the opposing cliff. From this vantage we skip the plentiful flat, smooth stones across the pool upstream. The couple leave, and we soon follow. A stretch of fine sand crosses a small feeder streambed to where a steep bank of gravel has overridden it. This clean stretch of the original bank hints at the fundamental river I long to engage—antebellum, antediluvian.

Reese has to cross the ford and direct me as I balance the car astride the wheel ruts and shoot for traction. We are soon back on the highway in a light shower, following the ridges that follow the curves of the land that lead the river. Elsewhere, roads are more direct, follow the waterways themselves, but here bottomland is scarce and precious. The only low road is the river.

Each landscape embodies its own geometric harmony. If a two-thousand-foot ridge in the Rockies appears only a few hundred feet high compared to higher peaks, a five-hundred-foot ridge in the Ozarks seems to rise twice its height measured against the many small hillocks before it. Walking either will require twice the effort you would guess. What distinguishes the character of a place is ratio, the description of its paradigmatic curve. The fractal equation of the Ozarks is gnarled. The oak leaf, the curl of the hickory's grain and the way its thick smoke twists in the moisture-saturated air of the hollows, the curve of one dry ridge after another, the path of the eddies at the blue end of rapids, the thread of the river channel and of syntactical connections differ from their counterparts elsewhere. This is what we look for when we travel to new places, what we miss about home while we are away. For many of us, many such patterning curves wait for the influence of the place, for the dialect, smell, or sight of home to fit like the curves of a violin to the jig that formed them.

This land has formed its people more than the reverse. Below the frost line, behind the homogenizing influences of the unrelieved landscape and uninflected dialect of the encompassing plains, the fifty-four-degree mean of their emotional tenor remains. I can talk to these folks, I find. I pick up the rhythm if not the accent when I return, and take away some comfort, if only by convincing myself I'm well out of it.

"There's real poverty here—people in pain," says the woman at the Conoco station. What makes her tell *me* this?

Standing in line to pay for gas, I'm behind a stringy man with a four-day beard, a wool hunting cap, flannel shirt. Union-suit red protrudes at the rolled-up sleeves. After he's paid for cigarettes and left, she holds her nose and shrugs at me, as if in apology. The man was fragrant of sweat, leaf mold, and tobacco, familiar smells. After he leaves, she mentions bathing habits, and I say something about a hard day's work.

"Well," she says, "some folks around here bathe maybe once a week."

"Whether they need it or not," I add, the punch line of an old joke.

I wonder if she is older than me, my age, or younger. She appears centered in that fathomless age of a worried adulthood that arrives early and stays late. How's business, I ask. She says the rain will mean missed mortgages, kids hungry. The national parks have added tourism to logging, farming, hunting, and barter—the mainstays of the local economy in the fifties. Off the river, away from the parklands, I wonder as I drive away, how much has changed? The woman doesn't say anything about her own condition. The proximity of hard times is manifest in what I call the hurt smile, in the way she apologizes first and questions later.

A time for everything: bath Saturday night, church Sunday. Pork should be killed in the light of the new moon.

Ten years ago, I made my first visit back to the area in over twenty years. My accent had been shaped and reshaped by stays in North (that is, black) St. Louis, laid-back California, and mostly the Pacific Northwest. I was enjoying hearing mannerisms I remembered from members of my family, verbal tics I find in my own speech after three whiskeys.

"Yessir they call practically anything with a flat bottom a john-boat, but it ain't. You can go along pretty well upriver with them new jet outboards, but let that motor go out on you and it ain't but one thing to do—stand in the middle of that river and holler for help. No way you'll paddle it. May as well throw a piece of plywood in the water and stick a motor on it."

He made johnboats at the Park Service visitor center. I had just come two days downriver and was preparing for a third. He built one or two boats each summer, stopping often to talk with visitors, ex-plain the history of the craft.

"How'd you come down? Canoe? That's the only way to see the river. That's all this here is, a canoe flat at both ends. Two young fellers your age could make ten, twelve mile upriver in a day of poling, not trying too hard. Carry half a ton of grain and two men with supplies downriver in four inches of water. That's what the old-timers used them for. Carried the wounded in the war. Nothing fancier than you see here—red oak and yellow pine."

He pointed to the struts and the hull.

"Old-timers only asked one thing, whether it was a wagon, the gristmill, this boat: 'will it work.' A johnboat worked and they used it a long time before roads. Course there's one thing you can't do with these like with those aluminum boats and that's to trailer it? This is made to stay in the river. Maybe take it out and treat it."

He gave me the proportions of linseed oil and other ingredients to treat the hull so it wouldn't end up in the same shape as the display boat they'd left sitting out at the ranger station.

"Dry rot. You try to move that one and it'll come apart. But in the river you can carry in it, pole upriver with one of these poling paddles." He points to a long narrow paddle carved out of dark wood. "I carve them out of sassafras. Here's a piece. Smell that when I shave a piece off here with the draw knife?"

Sassafras smelled the way sassafras smells, like candy, root beer, or toothpaste depending on the taster. He told me much I already knew and much more I didn't. About johnboats. About woodworking, carving away from your body (the bandage on his left hand the result of him forgetting that first rule of hand tools). About his son in my old stomping grounds along Oregon's Umpqua River. How the boy wanted to come back to help his old man, but there was still no coming home because no matter how bad the economy of the lumber industry, the Northwest at least *had* an economy. About using the sculling paddle to work the johnboat up to the deep, still, milky blue pools in the river where trout waited in the cold among the dozens of other species of fish there—how one stirs with the short paddle as if stirring soup, leaving the other hand free to cast. About the unique leaves of sassafras—three basic shapes, lobed, unlobed, and double lobed, growing on the same tree—and that they were the thickening and flavoring agent known as filé.

I hadn't known that, though I knew that it was supposed to be unlucky to burn it, especially for one's mother, rather like stepping on a crack for urban kids. But the exchange of information was secondary. As Whitman says, "Only the lull I like, the hum of your valvèd voice." We are not asked to believe that the dogwood was cursed for being the wood of the true cross, the shape reflected in the flowers, nail stains on the petals. Or of the Judas tree, that the shame of the betrayer hanging himself on its relative causes the white blossoms to blush, giving it its American name of redbud.

I did gather some practical knowledge, however. The curve in the river I'd negotiated the day before was the downfall of most tourists, providing a kind of cottage industry for local teens who would dive in the clear pool at the bottom of the rapids to retrieve cameras, camping gear, and watches. I'd let it be known that my grandfather was a blacksmith and that I had relatives still living in the area (though long out of touch), so I was brought up to date on the changes in the interregnum. People were ambivalent about the necessary tourism industry, which brought not only desperately needed dollars, but tourists who thought folks "quaint," stray dogs, a market for drugs other than local moonshine (a folk art demonstrated at another park), and several tons of trash in the river.

"The Park Service has a fish fry ever fall. Admission, a bag full of cans and bottles from the river. Folks gig them like frogs where they collect at the downstream ends of the pools—same principle as placer mining—and the rangers supply the fish. Ever been to a fish fry? Best fish you ever eaten. Get a drum of shortening to just under boiling, clean the fish, score them down the side?" (demonstrating here on his bandaged palm with two fingers) "and pop them in. They sink. And when they come back up they're ready, browned on the outside with the meat falling off the bones.

"But don't let them catch you throwing anything in that river or they'll fan you so fast . . ."

Here the tourist came out, the man who came to listen to the valvèd voice. I'd been savoring the idiom that makes questions of statements and vice versa and had smiled at the familiar shaping of diphthongs and semivowels, halfway between Deep South and Southwest dialects, that makes of one-syllable words two and vice versa, rhyming "Fords" and "forwards," "backwards" with "Packards," and replacing "fine" with "fan." The speaker noticed me smiling at the pronunciation.

"I mean that they will fiiine you. I can speak better than that."

And our conversation was over. We continued to talk, but the comfortable flow of stories and anecdotes was gone. For, shamefully, the tourist was me. Unlike Dante, I had no one to explain that I did not come merely for *diletto*.

The dogs are back at the campground, and so are the first big groups of campers. On our way to get firewood I meet Grunt, a bulldog whose ugliness only hints at his ferocity to other dogs. Already, nearby campers have staked their pooches to picnic tables to lick their wounds and pick, disconsolate, at aluminum-foil trays of food brought by their chagrined owners. I wonder how Grunt would handle the hounds.

The firewood is damp, the air saturated as the ground. Though I learned to make fire in coastal rain forests, it's deep dusk before a bed of coals shimmers in the fire pit. Fortunately, we don't have to use the smoky fire to cook. Whippoorwills and fireflies begin their displays in the dark river bottom while light lies on the hillside. This is not as unsullied as Jerktail Landing. Dog owners shout at pets and kids on one end of the campground, and the I, IV, V chord progressions of a Bob Seeger song retort from the camp of three young couples opposite. We make do, walking to the end of the campground—abandoned by everyone now but the hounds—where the tributary creek enters the river. We try to find the owl crying on the hillside. Sounds like a barred owl this time. It sounds close at times, but stays out of sight. Owls hate to be seen—the old predator's reserve.

When we return, the fire is smoldering and smoking and demands more fanning, blowing, and eye-smarting smoke in the face before it will burn. Eventually persistence rewards us with a blaze that just gets going in time for Reese to go to bed. Building it and fanning it and a few minutes of gazing at it have been our evening's entertainment. I sit up to enjoy the flames a while longer and make periodic forays outside the light as I begin to hear faint echoes of thunder. No lightning is visible in the west. I throw a couple more logs on and wait.

We have a good "fire of wood," another anachronism of speech that survived here. I am enjoying the luxury of it because I didn't have to cut it. I roll other localisms around in my mouth as I sit sipping water. Ozarkers use E. B. White's rule from *Elements of Style*.

"Write from nouns and verbs," he says. Okay, I hate to wood-cut but I like to fire-build.

It still is thundering, so I stay up. Full dark is over us, no moon, river mist darkening the sky, though portions of the hill are visible as a cityscape of firefly lights. The river sucks loudly and I think of the twin vortexes, the low-water bridge mirroring the eels, the many whirlpools forming and drifting off in the dark water only twenty or thirty yards away. A johnboat returns upriver from the search. It circles a low, brushy island at the creek's confluence and is joined by another. Two men are in each boat.

"Did you see something yellow in those branches?"

The reply is indistinct but dismissive. Both boats move upstream to the landing. In the silty water the spotlights create inverted funnels underlying the boats like a medium—as if the boats were buoyed by light. The river is clearing slowly, but more rain will cloud it again.

More thunder sounds.

The spiral's mysteries are lifelike. It appears in organisms—pinecone, crosshatched acorn cap, grain of wood, bone, and seashell. Its mathematical equations mimic organic processes, produce Mandelbrot sets and twistors—easier to hear in the night sounds than to visualize. Not the whirlpool's shape alone defines it, but its various sound dimensions, slurp and echo, call and response.

Twistors, points in an imaginary space mathematicians create of complex numbers, lack mass or dimension. They make up for their inadequacy by impinging on the surface space of quotidian existence in flowering complexity as concatenations of helical lines. Projective geometry, this is called. Trying to imagine complex space, we imagine ourselves in our dimension-poor reality as bugs on the surfaces of balloons and all sorts of other allegorical creatures. Water scooters come close to living in a two-dimensional world, but we'd have to be reflections on the water's surface to be two-dimensional. Each ripple in the surface tension would be nothing to us. We would ripple with it. Even the stretching and shrinking of the surface would be invisible, for all our visible landmarks would stretch. Then a whirlpool stretches our two-dimensional world into a third dimension. Reflections break apart. A hole appears.

I remember the woodsman before me at the Conoco. The world of the rural poor fronts a host of insecurities the "information age" urges us to explain away. I rent my canoe with my credit card, live in the information world, but I can't forget my other reality. We have a projective economy, Plato's shadows on the cave wall. Children grow up believing milk comes from plastic jugs. They find the warm product of a cow's wrinkly teat "gross." Still, in that ontologically stubborn world that persists despite our theories, something must die for us to live. We can replace all the rodents, bugs, fowl, snakes, microbes, grasses, flowering plants, and what-have-you in a field with a single crop, but it subsists within much narrower ecological limits. And so do we.

Which is the real world? Yes, it's all relative. Relative to what? Where is the C we tend to forget stood for the Constant that proved Einstein's equation? Respect that river, the locals say. They're reminding me that C also stands for Consequence.

The fire echoes water's movement, runs down in an image of chaos moving across the face of the bed of coals. Though I have already taken off my watch and promised myself not to look at it, my wandering thoughts are evidence enough of the time by my body's clock. It's truly late, and I will not stop the rain from coming by watching for faint flashes to the west. I feed the fire with twigs and dried leaves from a flood-downed maple for light enough to walk into the bushes for a piss. I glance at the sky again.

The silent owl launches from one of the overhanging cottonwoods. I see the mottled white of its wings and belly. The swimming motions of its wings—what swimmers call "the catch"—disturb the thick air as little as possible. The fire underlighting it, the owl corkscrews through the air. Its wings appear to circle the body like twin blades of a propeller, the twist in their design presaging their movement, as the maple keys now popping in the fire were shaped to score their helical flight. Most societies consider owls death's harbingers. They are moth-like, silent, confused by light, creatures of the vortex: like the doo-dlebug, gatekeepers.

No spiral effect tonight, no motion.

When the storm comes, I cheat and look at my watch. It is 3:00 A.M. A heavy rain falls for a few minutes, settles into a long shower as I doze, wake, feel for puddles on the tent floor, and listen for rising river water, then go back to sleep. Enough rain to keep the river from falling or clearing.

Falling

The feet of the screech owl burnt together with the herb plumbago is very good against serpents.

Pliny, *Natural History*

Next day I . . . ordered him to be plung'd thus bound into an
hogshead of water all of a sudden . . . but this had scarce any
effect because I neglected to blindfold him. . . . I contriv'd a
byspout from a Current of water which had a 20 foot fall. Thus
[by use of a cart] I kept him under this vast pressure of water for
15 minutes. . . . He who being blindfolded . . . came whistling
singing dancing and merrily leaping along . . . was fain to be
carried home in a Litter.

Treatment for "a fiery zeal for religion" in *Some Observations on
the Cure of Mad Persons by the Fall of Water* by Patrick Blair, 1725

  sharisí tivatashátaw vwarisítivirisi.
  varasáta varashita watí savarashataporáti sítiverisi.
  varasatalavarí shíta situvarayati tuvalisítalishi
  warisi takalasha talisí tawaray tatavatasay shata-varisiti.

Transcription of neo-Pentecostal glossolalia in
Tongues of Men and Angels, by William A. Sanan

AN OWL TAKES OFF FROM A TREE UNDERLIT BY CAMPFIRE and provides an epigraph to galvanize an entire chain of thought. An owl I observed in winter, dumped into air by the breaking of a snow-laden branch, seemed embarrassed, as if even such graceful and efficient fliers as owls are often uncomfortable with flight. Consider that the loopy woodpecker trapezing between wingbeats, continually launching itself along, is poised always at the edge of falling.

Swimming is easier, even for birds. Flesh floats in water. I once watched a cormorant inside a Pacific wave backlit by sunset. Trapped in my memory like the small creatures sealed in amber, it swims through the green glass of that wave, its underwater flight caught in the brief gleam of light through wave along with its prey, a sprinkling of smelt. Such suspended moments seem to lift whatever I'm watching out of context. This is the power and the danger of photographs.

I have in front of me photos of the congregation of the Dolley Pond Church of God With Signs Following. Taken in the Tennessee hills of the late forties or early fifties, the people resemble our Ozark neighbors in their dress, and the general air of grim rural poverty that clings to them. The communicants, preserved in the attitudes of religious transport, sprout handsful of snakes—copperheads, rattlers, and water moccasins. Some wear them looped over their heads and seem oblivious to the snakes' presence. One rawboned woman's sunken cheeks imply she's missing all her back teeth. She stares with a faint smile at the tangle—two? three?—in her hand. In two photos, women lie unconscious on the floor, the dark-suited preacher kneeling above them, laying his hands on them, victims not of snakebite, but of rapture. These are snake handlers.

Snake handlers get little good press. The minister of one of the first congregations died of a bite soon after a filming session, which seems to have left your rank-and-file snake handler suspecting Divine Providence frowned on filming the sacrament of the handling. Consequently there are few images of their practice. Fewer yet contradict one's initial impression—yet another bizarre cult bred in the backwaters of American culture. Though there were snake handlers in the Ozarks when I was a child there, it was mostly the more subdued kind wherein the demonstration is solely the responsibility of the minister— a snake-wavin' preacher. I was sheltered from such colorful individuals. The faithful are rumored to drink poison and stick their hands into blowtorch flames.

In defense of the snake handlers' orthodoxy, they could do worse than appeal to an authority so organic, local, and final. Snakes might be less likely to attack a person with a clear conscience. They're as trustworthy as the theory behind lie detectors. Besides, the snake is more likely to be objective than the technician *ex machina*—that little man behind the lab screen we keep trying to ignore. There were so many snakes in the Ozarks, it was hard not to become fascinated.

My aunt fondled snakes, but that was simply a morbid attraction. (She also stuck her hand in a fan to see if it would really cut.) Closer to sanctified status was the local man who truly loved snakes. He stacked fieldstone next to his cabin, and left a crack under his door unstanched in summer so his friends the snakes could come and go. He described his home; I was never allowed to visit. Like me, he believed coral snakes occurred this far north. He claimed he could pick up rattlers. Organized snake handlers, he said, were asking for trouble and disturbing the snakes they used, while he was living on equal terms with them. "Just like people. You let them be, they won't bother you. Well like most people, if you know what I mean." His fascination was not dogma, but more personal, a translation of the old obsession of the Egyptians, for whom the snake was an emblem for thought—consider the electroencephalogram.

Though I don't know the passion of snake handling, I might, on my mother's evidence, have a certain insight into how the snakes feel. Pressured by "Holy Rollers" (as we called Pentecostalists) to attend one of their services, my mother took me along. I was still in diapers. Their charming rituals included faith healing, pre-millennial testifying, glossolalia, and what the poet Richard Hugo called their "annual violent sing." Plain, down-home folk call it shouting your hair down, and it happens weekly or oftener. It's not snake handling, but it's plenty exciting. Seized by the spirit, my mother's friend snatched me from her arms and flung me into the air with some sort of ululation. I think my mother ends the story with me sailing through the air spread-eagled with my eyes wide as saucers. It's hard to understand her through her laughter. I imagine a kind of hillbilly Sistine chapel—one cherub executed by Thomas Hart Benton floating alongside the woodstove chimney and pine rafters, not knowing whether he is falling or flying. So with the snakes in the photos. They seem suspended in attitudes as impossible as the people's.

A different testimony of the Ozarks made itself known to me after a recent camping trip. I was driving away from a campground, noticing how the sassafras grew in cuts made for the access road. As a child I pulled saplings and chewed the roots. Suddenly, from the green wall of undergrowth, through the blur of moist heat, a red-tailed hawk took flight across the road. Clutched in its talons, the reddish yellow tinge of a copperhead writhed. In the seconds it took to cross in front of my windshield, I registered the motion of the snake as a Persian script. Its pattern burned into my vision as a moving light will trace lines on a dark-sensitized retina.

The motion, having writ and moved on, I could almost retrace from memory. But not quite. Herein lay its power for me—that I could not reconstruct it. I could recognize this as mine among all the other messages of time and movement: bug tracks in mud, termites under oak bark, the ampersands and exclamations of water behind river boulders and the dissolving and reforming portraits of the world that first shaped me as seen in the shadows of windblown foliage. This one message I could neither ignore nor decipher. Called and rebuffed.

Perhaps if I had remained. . . . In that country people still know who they are, though they are as often abashed about it as proud. Would I have thought twice about the message written before my moving car? Perhaps the place would not have needed to speak to me. The snake's movement against time and death would have been written in my bones and nerve fiber by the food and air, from having first been drunk on local liquor, from having a first sexual encounter under the same canopy of leaves with a girl grown from the same red earth with whom I would have written the same script in the dry leaves of some past fall, spoken its glossolalia. And had children the same. And been preached to and taught the same. And fished and eaten and loved and hated the same.

Falling, the movement of snakes, of water, of leaf shadows striking three-dimensional patterns into the *tabula rasa* of the dusty path—hypnotic. The cat scaling a straight wall, the hawk stooping—these are essays in abandonment, lessons in falling. They could be carrying messages in the waves of their bodies. Loosed from gravity, their movements serve no purpose, unless it's that redundancy the information theorists tell us is necessary to separate message from the constant background "noise" of the universe. Tongues loosed from the mouths that once held them, they could be speaking the gossip of God.

This is why boys throw cats in the air. Perhaps why they shoot at birds and throw stones and sticks (and knives) until their arms are sore. The pure useless beauty of flight and falling. Once or twice I've seen flying squirrels drift out of a distant tree. Unlike a bat competing with nighthawks for evening insects or chasing my fishing fly past my head, the flying squirrel constantly adjusts for the drag of its un-aerodynamic hair. Common gray or red squirrels in free fall are as impressive. They fall, and this is the beauty of flight.

A boy is drawn toward darkness and light. Snakes capture this draw, as do water and wells, this fascination with danger and falling. A snake with two tails resolved into one eating another. My parents ran them off with thrown stones.

I wasn't called to touch snakes but once. Walking with my mother, I saw a copperhead in a brush pile. I pointed it out to her, but the

golden leaves on dead branches disguised it. So I reached for the fat,
flat head where it narrowed to a neck before spreading into the puffy
body. My finger was inches from the snout when my mother finally
focused on the chestnut back pattern and snatched me away. The
snake, full and sleepy, thrashed into the brush pile. That was my only
experience with snake handling—other than garter snakes—but the
principles held. Like attracted like, my composure, my mother's fear.

Of course, this isn't statistically valid—the gods do not suffer all
fools or idiots. The parents of the hydrocephalic boy from our church
picked up with a more fundamentalist congregation and stopped his
treatments. He died. "Waterhead, waterhead. Nyah nyah nyah," the
children cry. Then the spastic boy in school started to pinch me,
though I wasn't part of the group of town kids who made fun of him.
The mean kid lived.

For a child living in isolation, a trip to town is the corollary to the
city kid's camping trip. From our isolated cabin, I had taken only the
first steps into the local community: baptism, two years in local schools. I
left the area at eight. Had I stayed, I might have been the first
generation of my family to blend into the culture of the area. As it
happened, I learned the human landscape elsewhere and differently,
built an eclectic edifice of Ozark sandstone, California stucco, and
Northwest cedar shakes. The same for my dialect, accent, values. So I
have very little claim to speak to the culture of the region.

And yet, the Ozarks were colonized by so many migrations that my
family may be the paradigm of the Ozarkian, the eternal immigrant—
the visiting Osage, the fleeing Shawnee, Tennessee and Kentucky
woodsmen, Germans and Russians, veterans of the war of 1812, of the
depression—coming for land cast off by other tribes, by the government, by mining and logging companies with no further use for it.

My grandfather, blacksmith and master machinist, came from England. He had worked in factories and foundries all his life, and I
guess he wanted land. He lived well in retirement, keeping eighty or
so acres, pasture and forest. I remember the house and farm as man-

orish and well kept, though it was ridge country, poor soil for a
working farm. My grandmother directed its upkeep, Himself being
away so often in the cities where the work was—St. Louis, Birming-
ham. I knew only the jovial old man, still so strong I could believe he
used to shoe draft horses suspended from a sling. I believed he let
them kick themselves away from him as he held the business foot. He
had a white shaving-brush mustache. He went helpless with laughter
when I crawled into the fireplace in my hateful Buster Brown suit,
and wouldn't let my mother punish me for it. On our walks he'd give
me one of the peppermints he claimed masked the pipe smoke on his
breath from Grandmother. I can't imagine him kissing her. If I ever,
ever bit my mother's leg again when I should be taking my spanking
like a man, he'd pull my teeth with blacksmith tongs. He promised.
Of my four grandparents, he is the one my mother mentions most
often. I know she loved her own father and missed him in some
private way only daughters can.

Grandpa Homer had the gift of falling. Lay preacher, singer in the
choir, there was some hint he'd led a different life in England. Maybe
the United States was the land of opportunity for him, maybe a
convenience. I think of him as Saul, one who had made peace with his
past. John Keats, another Englishman, though not blessed with the
talent to be a blacksmith, spoke of "negative capability." Manifesting
itself in empathy (Keats was writing, not surprisingly, to his brothers),
negative capability means one is "capable of being in uncertainties,
Mysteries, doubts, without any irritable reaching after fact and reason." Grandfather, amid personal tragedies—the various failures of
his children, the death of his oldest son, separation from his family in
England, the increasing brittleness and dourness of his wife—played
joyfully with his grandson, and laughed as heartily at his own foibles
as at the world's. Religious, his was a fall into grace—literally.

The visible signs of our congenital maladroitness, the Homer lia-
bility to error, he carried on his hands. Having discharged his indus-
trial gig without serious accident, he lost two fingers and part of a

thumb working with his youngest son, my father, on the farm. My mother and grandmother told these stories with particular glee.

Grandfather Alfred to his son: "When sawing wood on the band saw, Robert, always use scrap wood to push the piece through. Never, under any circumstances, do this . . ."

. . . and sawed off his thumb.

Driving fence posts in the rocky ground, one held the post, the other swung the sledgehammer. It was Grandpa's turn to hold, and they were near the end. Dad was swinging as one does. After each blow, the hammer bouncing on the wood, you let it fall off and use the downward momentum to set up the next stroke. It is the easiest way to swing a heavy sledge for any time, a comfortable rhythm:

WHOCK! Thunk-a . . . (pause) . . . WHOCK! Thunk-a . . .

Grandpa: "I think that's far enough."

He lays his hand on the burred top of the post and—WHOCK!— my dad finishes the swing.

My father got to go for help. I imagine my grandfather tossing off the pain rolling across the bed while Dad hotfooted it the three, three and a half miles to the telephone at the Corridon General Store, lucky in the thirties to have one so close. He's supposed to have come upon a neighbor in a mule-drawn wagon who asked if he wanted a lift. "No thanks, my dad's hurt bad, I'm in a hurry."

Great animals, mules, but there's no hurrying them down a dusty road on a hot day.

Years later, I rode the school bus down that road to Corridon School—two rooms, eight grades. The driver had a mean and tender humor, asked questions like "You get lots of Christmas presents from Santy?" I said not too many, and he: "Don't worry about it, ain't no Santy Claus. That's for babies."

I knew that, I lied, as if I were just playing along. It was second grade. The same bus driver told me the teacher, Mr. Dunn, had been captured by man-eating cannibals in the Amazon. "Cooked him too."

"So how'd he get loose?"

"Don't know."

"How'd you know they cooked him?"

"He's Dunn, ain't he?"

Sonny MacNeil, son of the preacher, owner of a welding shop, the last time I drove through, picked up where the bus driver left off. If you stick your tongue on the metal handrail when it's covered with frost, it tastes really strange—nothing like it, he told me. He also taught me my first bawdy song:

> I went to town like a good girl should.
> That sucker followed me like I knew he would.
> Come and let me tell you what he done to me.
>
> I went to the store like a good girl should . . .
> I went back home . . .
> I went on my porch . . .
> I went to the parlor . . .
> I went upstairs . . .
> I got into bed . . .
> None yer damn business what he done to me.

I should sing it to my parents, he said.

I was gullible. Our ridgeland property was far from people and water, and one is a mirror for the other. These isolations mesh. Both shaped the land, and we stayed high and dry. Water continued to be an unseen mover in our land and life. The course of the people was as subterranean and intricately balanced, as stagnant and as rapidly rushing. I sometimes wished we lived closer to people, at others, closer to water.

I got something of my wish the times we moved to Ellington—the megalopolis of two thousand, the largest town in Reynolds County. We rented out the cabin in exchange for first one, then another house, both just outside town. I had visible neighbors for the first time: the boy with whom I explored the bluffs and outcroppings across the creek, the deaf shoe repairman who either wrote or pantomimed his messages. He'd growl, making a snarling dog of his right hand attacking the left hand and driving it away. "Your dog's been fighting again." Or he'd mime the other neighbor driving over in his cab (*the* taxi in our town, and for all I knew, the county), then knocking at our door. "The dog barked," he mimed. "The driver gave up [shrugged] and went away." Once, when we asked who was by while we were gone, he pantomimed driving and held up two fingers. This identified a local man who had bought a new truck, but always drove everywhere in second gear. "Can't figure out how to shift it, too used to that old Fordson," people said. They held up two fingers as he ground past, cranking the wheel hard, trying to miss the potholes. "Take it easy," my dad would tell him. "You can't hit 'em all."

One cold day my father took his work boots once too often to the tiny shoe repair shop on the main street. In the warm shop redolent of shoe grease and the woodstove, our neighbor studied the stitches, the cracked leather and flapping soles. Then he walked around the counter, opened the door of the stove, and pretended to throw them in. My dad sewed the soles back on himself with copper wire and a carpet needle.

With my new playmate I climbed the steep slopes descending to the creek that ran past our backyards. Granite outcroppings gave us a dizzying impression of height as we looked over our houses, our brothers and sisters playing in the yards below. I hung by my knees off a dead branch over the dry creekbed and got a dizzy look at the rocks on the bottom. The sound of my head hitting was surprisingly bell-like, or like the rhythm blocks we smacked together at school. It must have sounded like this to the school bully when he got a rock in the head for trying to push the "slow" boy from the seesaw. Kids said you could see his brain, but there was just a loose flap of skin under his crew cut.

I liked the slow boy. It was alright to say "slow." It sounded better than "retarded." Later, he must have been "special," or as cruel kids now say "a sped" (contracting "special education," and proving the human heart creative enough to keep us from becoming boringly kind). He was two years older but still in second grade. His speech, now that I know such things, sounded like speech of the hearing impaired. I loved the strange-spoken boy's courage, his confidence. People said a horse had kicked him in the head.

Walking with his brother and a friend from their parents' place up the road, Ricky was warned not to come too close to our house. Boys feared rousing our dog, Shadow, a German shepherd–Great Dane mix. "He bide me, I bide him back," said Ricky. "He bide me, that be last time he bide me." There was no anger when he said it, or when he gouged the flap of skin loose from the bullying boy's head. He was no-nonsense, and Shadow—a bully like most dogs—believed him, and showed more sense than the boy at school.

One of our houses in Ellington lay next to a game refuge. Deer watched us from the woods as my mother hung up clothes. They grew so tame, they would eat rolled oats out of our hands. Until the local butcher explained to us that, when alarmed, not only stags but does often attack one another and other animals with sharp hooves that can open a young child's chest "fast as pulling down a zipper," we were charmed by the way they would stand still as we picked bloated ticks from behind their translucent ears. Ticks, chiggers, and mosquitoes fed on all warm-blooded animals. Ticks are an evolutionary marvel, hanging on grass or trees in suspended animation until the perfect bouquet of carbon dioxide and butyric acid (the rancid smell in sweat) releases them onto their host. Then they go looking for a likely spot. Favorites were behind the ears, just inside the hairline, and wherever skin or clothing binds—waistband, armpit, crotch, crack of ass, or behind scrotum. The number and variety of Ozark insects testifies to the hidden reserves of water never further than a bug's flight or a deer's walk away. The humidity is midwestern, verging on southern, the frost season mild.

As I came out of the deep sleep of my early childhood, we moved back to the cabin—no work in town for my father. With machinist skills and epilepsy, he was supremely unemployable. My brother was old enough to follow me on my shorter forays into the woods and shared the indignity of the daily tick search. Climbing in their thousands, seedling ticks blackened our legs, and we ran for the house and doused them with turpentine. Still, many got past, and we were checked before bed.

One day as I watched a hummingbird test the window, pane by pane, I felt a thrill and looked down to find a hornet trying to fly off my arm, stuck to my skin by its stinger. *Vespula Pennsylvanica* look like yellow jackets, but larger and more aggressive, fat thoraxed, blunt as the old Hudsons named for them. They also differ from their cousins the yellow jackets by building round nests in trees rather than in the ground—and by producing a more painful sting. A huge red welt rose on my arm, but I did not hate the hornets until later, when I came to believe that they killed my dog. For the time being, I was still fascinated by them.

From outdoors, the hornets' nest on my grandparents' window looked like the wads of toilet paper boys at school threw at the ceilings. In cutaway through the sewing room window, its spiral maze revealed the comings and goings of the hornet hive, no discernible queen or drones. One Sunday, I took the stool from the pump organ, spun it till it was high enough for me to put my ear to the glass. The drone sounded like adult conversation in the next room when I woke from nap. The sound fit the hot, humid day. Distant thunder.

A heavy rainstorm—the kind that washes all the dirt from the screens onto the windows, then washes the windows clean—destroyed the nest. Smaller storms had washed parts away. The hornets rebuilt after these smaller disasters, like people on a floodplain. Their sideways mandibles ground like goats' jaws at well-cured bits of wood from the pile of boards out back. They worked this lumber, left over from the house, with as much care as my grandfather had. The Sunday after the nest washed away, I screwed the seat back down on the four claws gripping glass balls, and pumped away at the organ. Holding down two or three keys, I pulled and pushed the different stops. Finally, someone told me to quit or I ran out of energy in the still, still heat, the stagnant indoor air of summer.

When I wanted to escape the narcotic limbo of the forest atmosphere, I'd first ditch my brother, then head for higher ground. Down the dusty path, through the gate, squeaking hinges held in with so many bent nails the gatepost looked like a fetish, and up the rutted access road I'd ride my bike. My first bike, and this the only place I rode it. Only as far as the top of the hill, my mother would say. Far enough.

The ridge near the cleared, grazed-out pasture had a precious commodity: air. Still days, a breeze of convection washed like a spent wave just over the tops of the trees. Amid the second growth, a persimmon tree gave access to breeze and a view. The land dropped off toward Logan Creek, across from the ruins of my mom's folks' cabin, and rose to the ridge beyond—several miles of vista in the blue of forested distance. On crystal days I could see a further ridge, on cooler ones, the clots of mist rising out of intervening hollows. Once I climbed the tree to watch a column of smoke until my mother's voice, worried, came drifting the quarter mile to call me back. They were watching the wind in case we had to leave. Without car or phone, and without a local radio station, we had to plan escape early. High and dry. Our nearest neighbors, the Vales would surely have come for us in an emergency. Amid the brushy stumps, the sumac- and poison-ivy-infested stands of blackjack, we stood like the few pine seedlings, ready to reestablish tenancy on the tired soil. We were second growth. We could not afford any more failure than was our lot by accident of birth.

I was not long in the tree before I tired of the view, having searched the horizon for clouds, spotted the gleam from the Forest Service lookout tower on the highest, farthest ridge. It was visible as a tower only through my father's binoculars, used for spotting smoke and varmints like snakes, weasels, raccoons, and hawks after our chickens, or deer after our garden. As my parents explained thermodynamics, running around climbing trees was a better way to stay warm than to cool off. But I needed air, or I would stop generating heat and theories entirely.

My methods were admittedly unsound, but if they didn't dissipate heat, they at least vented the frustration of stewing in my sweat until dust and dirt balls formed in the creases of my neck and at my armpits and across my middle where the baby fat rolled up. Carpe Diem! First I'd cover up with blankets and coats to get as hot as possible, pulling a pillow over my face in a redundancy of smothering. When I began truly to sweat, I'd charge out and run around the house, feeling the air in my wet hair. My parents watched, shaking their heads.

> If they could not make their son
> sit still, they could let him run.

With luck, a rainstorm would come through in the afternoon, steaming off the dirt at first, then cooling everything before evening. My mother would strip us and hand us a bar of soap to go shower. We'd return blue-lipped to the doorway and stand partially out of the downpour on the sandstone doorstep, squeegeeing the water off with our hands. We stepped inside to dry off with a course, line-dried towel. In heavier thunderstorms, we stayed inside to watch the trees bend nearly double, their tops ready to whack the ground, setting off the thunder cracks.

Parents get lost. They lose their tempers in the heat. The metaphor remains fresh in a blacksmith's family. Heat was only one worry. The hydrocephalic boy died. My grandfather came with the news that my mother's father had died. Lightning, they said, had blown a boy out of his shoes. It was the McCarthy era, though my parents scoffed at the idea of "Communists behind every bush." I had seen many bushes, and there were more often snakes in them. I said so and someone laughed and said, "Out of the mouths of babes." I thought this referred to my having got second prize in Sunday school for number of verses memorized.

My mother's look said more about the little child not being seen or heard for a while. She also remembered me sneaking away during nap time (strictly enforced, especially in the heat of the summer) to play in the Vales' visiting niece's wading pool, losing my privilege of going to summer camp. She had less patience than my father with religious affectations. "Tell the good ladies at Bible school I combed your hair with shit water," she'd say, dunking the big comb into the pot where my brother's diapers boiled and slicking down my cowlick.

The need to boil water is troublesome in summer, but it was either boil water or use purification tablets. Even wells weren't foolproof, and there were sick children to prove it. Drinking water slept in a pail, a long-handled dipper resting at the side. After a nap, I dragged a chair to the cupboard, climbed to the counter, and reached a broken cup from the top shelf. I noticed the three white pills dissolving in the bottom when I lifted it to drink—water purification tablets, I figured. When my mother came in from hanging laundry on the clothesline, I mentioned having especially clean water.

She put some foul stuff down my throat, followed by her finger, shook me up, and set me outside the back door. A foaming mixture of water and suds came out my mouth, and I didn't want to drink the tumbler of water she brought me. I don't know whether I swallowed my father's Dilantin or Phenobarbital. He'd broken his bottle and had put the last few pills in a cup on the top shelf. I didn't feel any effects from the drug, but the cure left me shaken.

Some hot days, I read. By third grade I'd read *Little Britches* by Ralph Moody, the original *Lone Ranger* by Fran Striker, and of course *Old Yeller*. The latter, rather than making me think deeply about loyalty, gave me an unreasoning fear of running into a wolf in the woods. I went more and more often to the edges of our forty acres, sometimes toward the neighbors' and sometimes toward the woods.

It was a toss-up. The persimmon tree stood near a fork in the access road. On one side the old wagon track went deeper into the woods, past the abandoned cabin and homestead. The other track went up to the dirt road that led to the blacktop that led . . . everywhere else— Ellington, Centerville, even Poplar Bluff.

I'd been to California to visit my mother's family. I had vague memories of it mixed with my early memories of St. Louis. I remembered trains, the smell, the speed as ours passed another with the scenery strobing behind, the tall black porters and waiters with silver trays. These were the Southern Pacific, the Santa Fe. I'd seen Texas, home of the Lone Ranger (more likely it was Wyoming I remembered): buttes, clouds red-brown as the land lying flat against the sky like Coke spilled on the glass tabletops at the Bowles Drugstore in Ellington.

In my nightmare I was smaller, a baby snatched from my father's hands like the lightning-struck boy. My father stood holding my shoe with the sock dangling out of it. He pulled the sock out, and looked confused. Between us, trains whisked his movements into frozen snapshots. He held something shapeless. The motion of the train cars created a strobe effect, like the strobes that drive brain waves, causing seizure. I called to him. There was not the usual noise of trains. A coupling between us hissed silence out of the hoses where the cars connected, and the silence was the heat taking my breath away.

I woke up thinking of my mother's dream. The night her father died, she dreamed he left on a long trip, saying he could not come back nor send for her. They'd had this conversation often, as he moved during the depression, looking for work, homesteading in Colorado, Missouri, sending for the family. My father did not die, but my parents were soon divorced. I could not know people are seldom equal to their dreams. A boy loses his breath, a man his family. I woke and was silent. We all lay—my mother and father and brother and I— losing water to the hot night, to the occasional mosquito. The land and air pulled it from us.

The last time I climbed the persimmon tree, the apparition of a breeze swayed the springy trunk. Brush, mostly sumac, grew on the logged-off hillside. Across the field stood a blackberry tangle criss-crossed with boards my father laid across the briers to pick berries for canning. I had several red, half-ripe ones in my pocket so the sourness could cure my thirst. The dry, bitter persimmons would suck moisture out of your mouth. They would not ripen till after the first frost, when we would open them, slicing down their soft seeds that would show the shape of either a knife, fork, or spoon inside. The breeze started the tree rocking, but I pumped harder, watching the distant blue line of the ridges sway with me. It seemed as if the whiplash, like the end of a fly rod, would shoot me into the ground. This would be harder than the fall from the dead branch into the creekbed, and into brush and briers. An anger arose in me. The heat? Some punishment? . . . I can't remember. I rocked harder.

The tree gave out first. At the end of one swing, it crackled like a bad back and refused to rebound. I hung above the ground upside down, nearly, farther up than I wanted to fall. I could only inch backward to where the exhausted bole of the tree straightened. It was ruined for climbing ever after. My feet were half asleep from being wrapped around limbs. Hotter than ever, I funny-footed it back to my bike.

Topsoil lay thin on the dome of the hill, thin as skin stretched tight over a joint. A gully came out of a little stand of trees on one side of the road, crossed a finger of pasture and a stand of saplings, and disappeared into the taller trees on the other side. I never saw water in it because it dried so quickly after a storm. The bed was sand and sandstone. The road simply crossed the gully, breaking down the sides and gradually lessening the dip until the next rain.

Weeks with no traffic to our place, and wind blew the new fill away, leaving the wheel-compacted strips behind. The wheel ruts became wheel ridges. I believe there had once been a culvert, but the sand swallowed it. Sinkholes will take whatever you throw into them—

even small ones you almost can't measure. Miniature black holes, they fatten on gravel, breed with sand, and bury larger things. They erode around boards, sheets of galvanized steel, till whatever you've been using to cover them tips and rolls away like an exhausted lover. The sinkhole eddies and adjusts away from its old center. After a rain, little vortices of sand appeared, looking like maps of storms. At their centers, what could have passed for large ant-lion traps. These were the sources of the rivers that underlie the Ozark Plateau.

Much of the water washed past too swiftly for the sand to absorb, downhill toward the hollows where it rose days later as mist. Past the roots of blackjack stands, it flowed to Logan Creek, cutting at sand, at clay, at sandstone and limestone and granite and washing the chips of chert along. Of that which sank, some probably met stone or clay and flowed along the seams to seep out further down the hill. Rejoining the flow, it swept downhill again until it reached the steeper slopes past my grandparents' old place. But always, it soaked into the porous ground, making underground rivers that cut caves and surfaced yet lower in springs, river pools, and shut-ins.

I like to think myself down the slow fall off that hill in Missouri, a piece of the local water taking a different path. Parts of me pissed away behind that bush slide past chert and the bones of tribesmen, past cast-iron stove lids and lead deposits to meet the creek and river below. I allow myself to believe I can follow the very broken and folded geology. My past casts up in mist over the ridges or folds into the tilting layers of rock. I slide backward, now deeper into the hillside, now siphoned up into some tilted conduit until, looking back up the well my grandfather dug, I finally see the stars through the barely rippling surface.

I may even indulge myself in the folly of imagining a small boy peering down into my single telescope eye, and long to call up some encouragement or advice. That is stagnation. Such a turn makes of the intricate circulatory system of water and mind nothing more than an elaborate Rube Goldberg device for moving around the marbles of molecules and memory. This is disturbing the fat old copperhead with malice aforethought, asking for a bite. The Ouroboros, the universal snake of time, bites its tail—symbolizing yin and yang, the continuity of life, the self-sufficiency of nature. In the Ozarks, it appears in the practical guise of the hoop snake, and uses its self-involved posture to roll away from trouble.

"Great Nature has another thing to do / to you and me," says Theodore Roethke, as he advises us to "learn by going where to go." And one of those things is to make us young once, to whirl us around, dropping us on rocks and creekbeds, until we learn like squirrels, snakes, cats, and water—like my grandfather—the marvelous trick of falling.

The Drownt Boy

And miles to go before I sleep

THE ROCK-'N'-ROLL COUPLES NEXT DOOR have a large tarpaulin covering their picnic table. Four poles hold the corners high enough that they've driven a pickup underneath. A fifth pole wedged onto the picnic table keeps the center high. Last night's rain filled the blue ripstop with about twenty gallons of water, pressing it tight across the camper top. The added weight is so much that they can't remove the poles, so they roll the water over the edges by pushing up on the bellying material. Eventually one of the poles breaks and the water spills out. One of the men is fanning up the campfire for breakfast and a woman is ruining a pair of expensive cowboy boots in the wet grass. They all look at me as if to ask what the hell I'm looking at. I grin and shrug.

Our breakfast is peanut butter sandwiches and fruit. For a moment, the thought of hot breakfast cooked over a fire is tempting. Our neighbors are now throwing kerosene-doused logs into the smoky fire pit and fanning them with frisbees. Hot coffee I can get at the store while we wait for our canoe.

Again, I stall, talk to the rangers, the concessionaires, listen to the reports of folks who've run the upper river in the last two days. Reese already thinks I'm taking it too easy. All my campfire meditation upon fronting nature, the difference between a river and a theme park, sounds thin now. Though a person in a life vest is hard to drown, it is not hard to get a concussion, break a leg, suffer exposure.

"We found the last three of them before the state boys," the man at the desk is saying. The canoe man is skeptical about using the helicopters and divers, plainly thinks the state would be better off paying locals to search the banks and the pools.

"How'd you manage that?" The ranger chuckles, good-natured.

Canoe man emanates silence. I sneak a look over the racks of plastic worms and shrink-wrapped Mepps lures. He gives the ranger a hard stare.

"Same as we always did," he says. "Our methods been known. Our ways been known, years."

Mark Twain described a couple of them. Thinking Huck and Tom drowned, the townsmen fired cannons from flatboats to make the corpses float up. A former classmate of mine worked for the Portland, Oregon, coroner. Each year when the fleet came upriver for the annual Rose Festival, she had to work overtime cataloging the "floaters" who surfaced thanks to the vibrations of tugboat screws. Shotguns will serve, or dynamite. Later, Tom and Huck have a crisis of conscience deciding whether to take the silver dollars the men float in loaves of bread, believing these will circle a submerged corpse three times. At my birth and my brother's, a doctor recommended taping on a silver dollar to avoid a herniated navel. Silver has power, as do steel, fire, and various animals and plants. A rooster in a boat is supposed to crow over a corpse, or certain branches locate a body in the manner of water witching. Some use mercury.

Maybe the man at the store had more practical methods in mind. Send teams of locals up the riverbanks where the body could have washed up. Use dogs. Follow the wild hounds. Look for buzzards in the trees, unusual concentrations of crayfish or eels in the water. I like the way he repeats "Our ways *been* known."

A fellow I call Tiny drives us upstream. If the upper river hasn't receded to normal levels, it may at least have cleared. Other canoeists have run it, and we have an idea of the hazards—a low-water bridge at Cedargrove, a two-foot wave that shoots across the stream from the flooded outwash of Welch Spring. We'll be running lighter without overnight gear, making the canoe more maneuverable but less stable. Disadvantages: the hollows are narrower, the S turns tighter, and the river faster. I've never been down this stretch.

Tiny was built for overalls. In farm towns all over the country desiccated men wear overalls so loose they're almost obscene, a white flash of fish-belly flank visible where the shirt works out of a loose flap of denim. Not so Tiny. He fills the overalls and his shirt tucks neatly in. He's round, clean-shaven, and just firm enough not to jiggle when he walks. He doesn't breathe hard when he lifts the canoe above his head. He's not threatening, thanks to a baby face and mild voice. He fits tight between the seat and the wheel of the van. Another group has rented canoes, but they are setting out later in the morning. We are alone in the van, and there's still a bit of mist hanging in the trees.

He's observant. He asks if this is our first trip. I tell him we've been here since Monday night, and canoed the lower part. When he asks if I've seen the river when it's running clear, I tell him I lived here as a child. He nods.

What's important is where my home place is—a way-back ridge road in the next county—who my kin are. Tiny doesn't know many people from that part of the country. Some of my elementary school classmates are from big families, and Tiny knows a few of these. I'm surprised to learn that the quietest boy in my first-grade class is someone "you don't cross," according to Tiny.

"Look here. You like cars?"

"Old cars?"

"Fellow up here's got a '52 Studebaker pickup."

The last one I remember belonged to our neighbor in Ellington. It would have been about 1958, the truck five or six years old. Mustard yellow, bullet-shaped, and low to the ground, it was the Buck Rogers pickup of the future. Others were bigger, more powerful, and had higher axles. Like that of two-fingers, his new Ford in second gear whining like a turbine at thirty-five.

"Sounds like some of those old boys," Tiny says. We keep our eyes peeled for the catfish snout of the Studebaker as we cut past a farmhouse on the rolling tableland. The owner must have gone into town. The yard is empty. Tiny has an early fifties Chevy and wants to know if I think he should get a bill for the windshield like the ones so many of the old trucks sported. I'm for it, so he proposes to sit down that very night and write to Whitney's.

We're crossing open fields, the top of a plateau. This soil is good for grazing and hay, the second-best land in the Ozarks and more plentiful than bottomland. If a farmer tills this land heavily—say for corn—he'll end up with a field full of chert and sand, sumac and "them other brush" as people used to say. If I were Tiny, I'd have my eye on a piece of plateau land.

"Good grazing land here."

"Yessir, I wouldn't mind me some of it. Run me some real fine cows."

Tiny goes off into his own reverie, rousing to point out a pair of pileated woodpeckers. Out of politeness, I assume (there being a child present), he calls them wood hens, rather than woodpeckers or woodcocks. Big, and common in the Ozarks as they once were throughout North America, they're important to local magic. I like to think that their success here is as much a function of the locals' respect for them as it is due to the favorable habitat—plenty of hardwood trees with their attendant parasitic bugs and grubs. It's illegal to own an eagle feather, but presumably one can still use the parts of a "Lord God peckerwood" for the traditional charms.

At the landing, Baptist Camp, a young man from Salem is trout fishing. Fishing with spinning gear and corn, he's caught two already

and pulls another out as we speak. The trout look healthy. I'm a bit
concerned about putting in and ruining his fishing. I offer to drag the
canoe downstream, but he shrugs it off. The fish are freshly stocked.
Dumber than rocks, they'll bite at anything. This offends my sensi-
bilities, but then, I've become effete. If he's fishing for food, he's
going about it the right way—efficiently.

In five minutes we are around the first turn. Isolated. This far up,
river fog still rides the water. It steams off into the narrow strip of sky
above low cliffs. Ribbons of old grazing field snake behind the trees,
bordered only by rotting fence posts, occasional stretches of zigzag
split-rail. It is too cold and wet for most wildlife. Even the birds are
silent.

But not inactive. Out of the mist, the occasional sparrow or black-
bird whirs mutely past. Above, turkey vultures patrol the widening
iris of blue sky. Carrion smells come strong from one or two willow-
covered bars. The bars, sandier than downstream, reflect less logging
damage. The forest is thick along the bank.

This morning even the unspoiled river threatens. It is cold on the
water, though the fog soon rises to high overcast. Vultures perch on
overhanging snags and we involuntarily duck. Theirs is an anointing
I would rather avoid. In local tradition their charge is to puke on the
incestuous. Vultures, harpies, owls, nightjars—winged reminders of
the world of consequence.

Where side creeks come in, narrow pools lie along steep banks. In
one of these, branches of fallen sycamores completely span the river.
We glide over two of them, the boles invisible in the murky water and
sky glaze. Fragrant islands of boughs rise around us. The sliding
current thrums them, leaves large as our heads minutely atremble. A
third sycamore lies at the surface, water slightly dammed up behind
it. I can see no way around. Though the current is slow, this is not
slack water. It would be hard work going back upstream—besides,

turning around in a narrow river is dangerous. We back paddle until I can hang onto a branch and consider.

One bank is steep rock, the other thick willow and flooded gravel bar. If we try to go around, we risk snakes in the thickets. Besides, it's a very hard portage. So we decide to go over. We paddle up to the bole of the sycamore, a scarce inch of spill covering it. Reese kneels behind his seat, and I lean back, so the bow of the canoe is high in the air. When we scrape onto the bole, the canoe is far enough along that the current keeps us pointing downstream. I was afraid we'd turn sideways on the trunk, and the current would glue us to the tree. Reese creeps further back now as I paddle and we inch forward. When Reese eases himself back to the bow, we should have moved enough that I can push us off using the paddle as a pole.

It doesn't work. We grasp the sides and try to scoot ourselves off. Finally, I have to creep forward as Reese paddles, and we slip forward slowly till we're free. The bottom of the canoe ripples but does not buckle. I only now notice that the flat bottom of this aluminum canoe is flexible, rippling as we shift our weight.

It's rapidly becoming clear the floodwaters have not receded on the upper river. We pass two springs, Montauk and one unnamed one, both gushing discolored water down flooded branches. The saturated ground has not yet disgorged its excess. This upper river as seen on the map is really the middle river. A few miles from here the Current appears from three springs in the middle of a meadow as a full-blown stream. The true upper river is all underground.

These narrow channels, sharp curves, and fallen trees are the makings of disaster. I am getting angry with the businesslike, well-coifed woman who consulted her computer after doing our paperwork. Surely someone reported the blocked river. Unlike Tiny or the canoe man, she was reassuring. I begin to remember a vague hesitancy about Tiny, as if he wanted to tell us something.

I soon shake it off. We're committed. After the fog lifts, it is easier to see what's approaching. We alternate between chutes and long,

flooded pools where the slow-moving water writhes with crosscur-
rents. We fight to avoid flooded willow stands and snags. Many of the
pools have two outlets, the main course and a secondary one. With
the water this high, they're hard to distinguish. A broad sheet of
smooth, fast water leads to a tangle of root wads in a narrow back
channel. We paddle hard for the main channel. A tree has fallen from
the steep bank into the outside of the curve where the water is deepest and swiftest, and where the river tries to take us. Navigating
between tree limbs and sudden boulders is tense work. We don't relax
until we shoot back into a long, quiet pool.

At the head of the pool, we crack the five-gallon bucket where
we've stowed our dry clothes, Reese's camera, and our lunches. My
car keys, wallet, change, and other pocket paraphernalia ride in a river
bag tied to the thwarts. Also tied in with the bucket is the collapsible
water jug about half full. I'm happy we don't have a full load of bags,
tent, and other camping gear. Overhanging branches have less to grab
at. Once or twice we've had to bend down and let the limbs claw our
backs as we shot under.

The high haze lets through a diffuse light. I get out the sunblock
and dose up. Reese disdains such caution. He's also getting hungry. I
want to hold out for two more rapids, hoping this will bring us close
to the Cedargrove Bridge, the halfway point. I doubt it. It's going to
be a long day.

Near the end of this pool, there's a deep hole, right at the top of a
series of esses. At this point, gravel bars alternate with the older, more
extensive sandbars. I angle for the outside curve of the pool where the
current picks up. I'm trying to see downstream. There are several
root wads, but they seem to lie toward the inside curve, away from
the main current. All I have to do, being steersman in the back, is stay
in the current. Reese has been practicing having the paddle on the
outside of the curve to push off. He is our lookout for boulders or
limbs of downed trees sticking out of the water.

"We're floating into a big limb" he says for the fifteenth time this morning. And we are. It's sitting in the current, centered in the pool above the beginning of the chute. Right where we want to be. Obviously part of a large submerged tree, it juts above the deepest part of the pool, throbbing back and forth at the urging of invisible undertows. I take a minute to make sure there's room downstream of it and back paddle to point the nose of the canoe away from it.

"It's coming right at us."

"I see it," I say. "We're okay . . ." the last words I say for several minutes.

The bow of the canoe with Reese in it clears the black limb, much thicker than I thought. The next stroke should shoot the canoe forward, but a powerful eddy sweeps us sideways, underneath the limb. Slow-motion time begins. I worry about going into the chute sideways and sweeping up against the first of the root wads. I whip my paddle around and present it in both hands as if I were countering a blow with quarterstaves.

The force of the eddy and the motion of the heavy limb knock the paddle out of my hand and into the water. The limb keeps coming at my chest. I finally realize I am going to be raked out of the canoe. I try to flip out backward without overturning.

For Reese in the front, it can have been only a couple of seconds since I said we were okay. When the limb catches me across the chest, it forces the breath out of me. I deflate, squawk, and go over. Reese turns around to see what I'm blowing about. My last sight before I go under is the canoe spinning over from the combined motion of my legs dragging across the gunwale and Reese turning in the bow. The water ships in, and Reese slips smoothly into the dark current, still dutifully clutching his paddle as he drapes his arm over the edge of the canoe. Then I plunge into the cold, smoky water, falling into the vortex of the eddy.

Storms

Their appearance was like burning coals of fire, and like the appearance of lamps: it went up and down among the living creatures; and the fire was bright and out of the fire went forth lightning. And the living creatures ran and returned as the appearance of a flash of lightning.

Ezekiel 1:13–14

FALLING IS BEAUTY. Cherry blossom, water, and hawk achieve their heart-stopping beauty at the instant of descent. The fall is freedom from gravity. The falling child thinks he is flying. Cats, snakes, and flying squirrels are not fliers, but graceful descenders like the letters *g* and *y* with flourishes on their tails. Leaves falling, the fall of the year, and the fall of light upon upturned faces all invite us to celebrate Aristotelian purgation. The lightning stroke is Blakean terrible beauty. The fall of water or a chisel sculpts stone into beauty.

Not so, a man. Not so the land, a tree, one's father. When I was between six and nine, living in the Missouri Ozarks, both the land and my father were falling. My father because of his epilepsy (*grand mal*— the big hurt), and the land both because it was broken peneplain— heavily eroded tableland—and because it was logged, mined, and

farmed out. Both were unresponsive to treatment. My father continued
to have seizures (the word itself redolent of medieval ideas of posses-
sion) and the land grew chert, some corn, thin pasture, and blackjack.

Blackjack is a second-growth tree, a scraggly oak commercially
useless except to be made into charcoal in tepee burners stacked high
with ricks meant to cook in a controlled smolder. When the pine and
the white oak have been cut, sumac, sassafras, and blackjack have
their place in the succession. They provide cover, limited erosion
control, and shade for the slower-growing trees that eventually either
shade-out or strangle their nurse trees. In this, they are like certain
spiders, the female eating the male, then mummifying herself with
her eggs until they hatch. The hatchlings secrete juices that kill her,
liquefying her inside her exoskeleton and allowing them their first
meals—an odd kind of nursing.

My mother lost all her hair while pregnant with me. It's usually a
sign of malnutrition, especially protein deficiency. Often such babies
are born with health problems, sometimes retarded—unless the fetus
is strong enough to wring the nutrients from the mother. The new
generation devours the old, eventually, as every parent will attest, but
in marginal land, marginal people are closer to this threshold. The
margin stares them in the face. Through mining and logging, the
land early settlers heralded as teeming with life became marginal.

Am I harping? Are you tired of marginalia? Sorry. Certain words
insist on themselves. The border between places or states of being is a
"mark." The words have the same root as *march.* A person's place was
once measured by how far one's feet could carry one—usually in a
day. The harvest of grain allowed "the outer marches" to extend.
Men, and groups of men, soldiers, could carry enough stored energy
in seeds not to have to live off the land for days at a time. Then horses.
Then conquest. Then war. Then more marginal land.

Other words. *Acre* comes from the Greek word meaning to drive—
as in the amount of land a man could drive an ox to plow in a day—
a drive of land. *Agent:* a driver.

Poverty is a powerful agent within the boundaries of the Ozark Plateau. No amount of reworking could make our land commercially viable. The Forest Service paid us to speed up the forest succession with a pine-planting program, and a mining company bought exploration rights. Neither provided an enduring income, though they mitigated the need for assistance—commodities and Aid to Dependent Children, what the black kids in St. Louis used to call AAYdeesee. Authorities on poverty say its most common effect is shame. African tribespeople whose bloated children have starved apologize to relief workers for their homes, for being poor hosts, not offering food. For a while, the land supported us, subsistence farming and the competing contracts—one to restore the land; the other to mine it.

Planes flew low overhead. We had grown used to the drone of the C-130 flying boxcars echoing through the sky thermals for what seemed like hours before and after they were visible in the sky above us. The sudden roar and sonic booms of jet trainers from Fort Leonard Wood rattled the top of the woodstove and shook soot from the chimney pipe. Now single-engine planes dangled cables with sensors like water-witching wands divining the secrets of the land below us. Then the pine seedlings came, and a new planting season.

So the pines could steal a faster march on the blackjack, we thinned the woods and girdled the standing trees. We notched the dark oak bark, revealing the surprisingly white layer of inner bark in a complete ring around the trunk. This kills the trunk because the cambium is the only living part. The trunk remains standing, the roots alive, sending up shoots at the base of the tree. The leafless upper branches give the seedlings more light. There is more water for the seedlings, too. Sheltered from the extremes of heat and cold, the soil held in place by the slowly dying nurse trees, the pines grow rapidly. In the forest, too, one generation feeds on another. In fifteen or twenty years, the pines form a respectable young stand with white snags standing about as after a burn.

Nearly thirty years later I went back to hills transformed. Like an

advertisement for forestry practices, the stands of shortleaf pine—
what I learned to call yellow pine—cover the old overgrown hilltops.
The seedlings we planted are thirty feet tall. The gray snags, shorn of
all branches, lay or stand like monolithic spires. When we replanted
twenty acres of our land, my father hired men to come with chain
saws and clear a path for the electrical lines. The curiously uniform
wood chips a chain saw produces stuck to the red flesh at their
waistbands, as they hauled the saws and gas and oil to the edges of
trucks. While they felled trees in a path up to the road, my father
girdled the blackjacks on the other side of the house with the double-
bladed ax. My job was to trim the watershoots from around the
stumps that kept the forest back a few yards from our fence.

My old ax was sharp. The first lesson of working in the woods is that
dull tools are more dangerous than sharp ones. A properly sharpened ax
is pointed at the heels—the edges of the cutting surface. If the stroke
goes astray, the sharp corner will stick in the wood. A rounded corner
will glance off and cut through any but a steel-toed boot. I once had to
help carry a man off a hillside after he cut himself with an ax. He kept
asking us to set him down so he could empty the blood out of his boot.

After the chain-saw men finished, and blackjacks stood girdled,
there was an open, naked feel to the place. The branches that had
been the squirrels' hidden highways now lay open. Several birds had
begun to build nests, and the shriveled leaves left them exposed to sun
and rain, as well as to jays, crows, and other nest robbers. A more
radical change was the open corridor between our cabin and the road,
about a third of a mile distant. The progress of the road grader on its
morning-down-and-evening-back route was not only visible but audi-
ble. Trees, people living near highways discover, are excellent acoustic
barriers. Now the sound of heavy equipment, cars, the trucks that
replaced the few mule-drawn wagons joined the planes in our world.
The mail carrier was a visible presence. Also obvious from our cabin
now was the arrival of the school bus—no dawdling in the woods on
the way home for me.

When the trees had been felled and limbed, the brush stacked for burning so it wouldn't be a fire hazard, a neighbor brought a draft horse to tow the sectioned logs to be sawed up, split, and stacked for firewood. In the frost of fall we were still lugging the wood. My father stacked, and I collected until he got too far ahead and began roving out to gather more pieces. Once a cord of the sweet-smelling stuff fell on me. My dad shouted and I ran, but several pieces caught me across the legs and I fell, more falling on top of me. The ground was cold. Always I managed to bang a finger between two pieces of wood—perhaps the congenital Homer clumsiness; I still do it. I expected being hit by the cordwood to hurt like that. The pain of bashing a cold finger travels up your arm, penetrating the pain of the cold and overlaying it with new pain. I was hardly scratched. I fell in soft dirt, and though my dad had to dig my legs out, I had no broken bones and surprisingly few bruises.

Whenever my father called out loudly, I froze. His seizures often began with a loud cry, and that sound—air forced from his lungs by the initial contraction of the chest muscles—terrified me at least as much as the seizure terrified our fundamentalist neighbors. The attacks were shockingly unpredictable. Reading a bedtime story to my brother and me, he stopped. We jostled him to go on. I still remember the sentences he had just read: "They were flying down the road. If the old flivver could have, it would have sung 'She'll Be Comin' Round the Mountain.'" Singing a hymn at church with my mother playing piano we heard the singing stop, my father's gasp. My mother and I looked at each other and she went to him.

My father, my brother, and I were taking a sponge bath in a pan of hot water before going to church. He collapsed into the woodstove and sank to the floor. I didn't want my mother to come in to see him, vulnerable and naked. He flopped like a landed fish as the seizure shook him. She would make us go into the other room. His legs ran air, sprinting a dream landscape, then stilled. We wouldn't be going to church this week. Waking, he was always groggy. A red burn surfaced between rib and hip. I didn't want her to. . . . If he was not possessed by the devil, we were. Seizures meant fights. Meant us kids banished, whiny and complaining. For years I blamed my mother for the fights, for the air of disapproval, for her anger and fierce protectiveness.

Dad was collecting fence posts from the power-line clearing, and I had been sent to call him home for lunch. He stacked the straight poles made of the small trees, limbs, and quartered sections, pointed the ends with the ax, and carried them uphill a quarter mile to our garden. He was only about five six, but very strong from a lifetime of such work. When he cried out and collapsed, the impossibly large load of rough-cut fence posts he had balanced over one shoulder fell like pickup sticks, covering him.

I turned quietly and walked away. I started toward the house. I must have been seven. We were in the draw that ran between the house and the road, parallel to the road. Nearby, the pond watched behind its small earthen dam where I collected frog eggs and let them dry to a slight stain on the rocks. Above, the dry creekbed stretched toward the crest of the hill. An old oven grill and a battered pot sat on an outcropping of sandstone a couple of feet above a depression in the creekbed. This was my camp, next to an imaginary pool of water, where I turned my horse, Apache (played by our dog, Shadow), loose to graze. Tonto (my brother, Dave) was helping me track down my colleague, the Lone Ranger, to tell him I was the one other person who escaped the outlaw attack on his ranger troop, like him left for dead in something called an arroyo, which, though I didn't know what it was, seemed from context to be something like a box canyon, only dustier.

This is where I ended up, though I started for the house to tell my mother of my father's accident. Later, I told her I forgot to look for him. On the way to the house, I had practiced how to tell her, without thinking of the right words. I may have gone to my camp to think of this. Maybe I did forget. We had a long talk, but I stuck to my story. To lie, one has to have passed through doubt.

The devil room and the ocean room had supplied this.

The ocean room was my version of Descartes's baker's oven. If I remember my anecdotes correctly, he sequestered himself in the oven until he arrived at the happy axiom "I think therefore I am." (For *axiom*, see the Greek roots *axios* "worth" and *agein* "to drive"; see *agent*; see *acre*.) The ocean room was my bedroom in one of the houses near Ellington, two years earlier. Painted light blue, it looked out from a slight rise over several fields of bottomland, the brushy margins of a creek, and a small airfield and hangar inhabited by a Forest Service spotter plane with a radial engine spoking out through its cowling. From my bed on summer evenings or during naps I saw only sky. The house grew quiet. No cars passed. The biplane no longer yowled through the valley. I could hear my blood powering through my ears like the sound of waves on a beach. The sky drifted off into distance with layers of nimbus. I began to feel the rush of my pulse knocking at my skin, as if to get out. If I lay there long enough, the pressure of my weight against the mattress and the pulse at my temples began to rock me as if I were on a boat. I was at sea.

Plainsmen fall in love with the sea. Having been in the forest all my life, I created a sea of the flat, shallow valley. I raised myself to one elbow. The forested tops of the hills, headlands, rose like islands in the sea of fields and pasture and the lawn washing up to the house. To get up was to wake my mother, sleeping down the hall, attuned to the first contact of my foot with the floor.

This led to the second level of doubt. If I could sense the sea where no sea existed, might I be imagining my mother? What if I wasn't imagining her, but she weren't my mother? What if nothing looked as I imagined it, and, when I looked away, it reverted to its original shape, one too frightening for me to see. Often adults stopped speaking as I entered the room, or made arch comments. Little pitchers had big ears and didn't know their cousins from Adam's off ox. When we looked for a lost tool in the yard, we had looked all over the devil's half acre. It would have bitten us had it been a snake. Even Shadow had intimations. Aware of some disturbance, he'd turn to look at his tail, then spin as if he could see the hidden order that made Van Gogh squint and Thoreau stand on his head. Staring into the blue sky, I glimpsed mosquito wigglers swimming in front of my eyes. For a moment I could visualize my mother and father as the strange crea- tures in the fairy-tale book. Then she walked into the room. Could she divine more than my slightest movement? I was so surprised, I swallowed the cat's-eye marble I had been sucking on so I wouldn't get thirsty and call for a glass of water—which, somehow, I couldn't visualize as anything but a glass of water. I drink therefore I am.

The more existential crisis of the devil room has to do with the same house, with moving out of the woods, the proximity of water, and how I learned to draw.

I wanted to draw airplanes. High up, the contrails of jets drew themselves along. The spotter plane roared in and out of the airstrip twice a day all summer. Cargo planes droned on and on like mon- strous horseflies. In the encyclopedia there were pages of pictures of airplanes—Navy Grummans with folding wings and swept-wing jets. The perspective of this incline of wings in the pictures fascinated me. I lay pencil or crayon against paper. The shapes firmly fixed in my mind, I began to draw with sure fast strokes, willing those shapes out, out the ends of the rapidly moving tip. What appeared shocked me— a feeble cross. To stop my screeching, my mother drew a cockpit and a propeller. Never mind that it was supposed to be a jet fighter.

Asked to draw my house in Sunday school I did no better. When I brought the drawing home, I noticed the sky looked wrong, a blue strip high above the tops of the trees. My mother knew better than to tell me it was okay, and tried to explain that the sky came down behind the trees.

In my view of the world, the sky stayed firmly above the trees. Behind the trees—more trees than I wished to draw—there stood yet more trees. No use pointing out to me that the sky appeared to touch the tops of the trees. I would point out that we could see it didn't really touch the trees because birds flew between the trees and the clouds. The clouds were between us and the blue sky. Besides, I was ready to argue, we were outside the picture, even if, to the people in the picture, the sky seemed to touch the trees. Showing me photographs didn't help, and my mother said something about stubborn little boys arguing.

"Okay," she said, "then leave it the way it is."

"But it doesn't look right."

"Then color in the sky behind the trees."

"But the sky is above the trees. It doesn't go behind them."

"Sure it does, look."

In the house in the valley, the sky stayed firmly in place outside the ocean room. The den, which became my room when I proved too restless a neighbor for my parents' side of the house, looked out on a hillside field. These windows were full of the earth wall of the hill. It was as if walking through the house were walking into the earth. Through the back door of my room a concrete-floored back porch sat above a real, machine-sunk well. The wellhead projected from the floor, a red pump with a freshly lacquered red handle. This was a conduit into the earth where the waters flowed—not bright surface waters, but obscure underground waters velvet as the lower ocean depths. Its phosphorescent denizens were illustrated (from *luster;* see *light;* see *Lucifer*) swimming the indigo depths of encyclopedia pages.

Probably the devil was what you'd see if your parents weren't hiding the truth from you, calling your rotten drawings good. If the devil were going to reveal himself, it would be in the den, dark, wood paneled, with shades instead of curtains. He would sneak in and touch your face in the dark and when you woke your mother wouldn't recognize you, like when she pretended she couldn't see you—only not playing this time. Someone had warned me about sleeping with my arm over the side of the bed. If you haven't heard it, don't think about it.

Nights are the worst, aren't they? Your parents are far across the house. The room is darker than dark. It is can't-see-your-hand-waving-in-front-of-your-face dark. You can drink only so many glasses of water. You sleep and wake terrified with your hand touching the floor. That hand reaching out of the shadows under the bed was inches from your fingertips when you woke. In the middle of the night a furred hand lightly brushes your face. Then it's a smothering weight, a disembodied limb, a small animal wrapped around your neck, its claws at your shoulders as you wake screaming. The Manx cat—the black one of course—loped its strange rabbit hop off the bed, my parents running from their room far, far across the house.

This was the devil room. Once I had suffered it, the second crisis of faith followed. In the overheard conversations of adults and in the hints, intimations, and glimmers from nightly Bible readings, a sense began to develop that the frightening fundamentalism infusing the hills was not all-in-all. "He who has ears, let him hear," says Jesus. It sounded good to me, a wink amid the dire quotations favored by fiery preachers.

This precocious bent, listening in on adult conversation, occasionally piping up, was a function of isolation. By my generation's standards, I was a deprived child. I had no television, few playmates, a sometimes limited diet, and toys that the guardians of public safety would not now approve—though my mother drew the line at a real gun with firing pin removed offered by a neighbor. I was blissfully ignorant of most blandishments of consumerism in the fifties, and so amused myself with reflection, observation, and eventually, reading.

When I look at books written for children before the twentieth century, I'm impressed with the diction. The vocabulary in Grimm's fairy tales doesn't coddle children. My parents read to us from books other than the Bible. The children's books, we read over and over as children prefer, until the child has the story memorized. A baby-sitter reading the story of Little Red Riding Hood—preferably the original gory version where the woodsman cuts the poor wolf open to let the spoiled little thing out—will be told, "No, the wolf says it like this. . . ."

I could fake it before I could read, turning the pages of my favorite story, *The Musicians of Bremen*, at precisely the breaks in the text. I still remember much of it. The cat with a face as gloomy as three rainy days, the donkey who'd taken his master's grain to the mill for many years, the other animals turned out by their masters for being too old to do their various jobs deciding to go to Bremen to become town musicians. For, as each of them decides, "I am said to have a very fine voice." The trip through the black forest (which I still assume looked very much like the Ozarks) ends with the animals losing their way to Bremen and finding themselves. It's precisely the way a story should end, with a twist that is not what the reader is led to expect, which allows for self-discovery. It even ends with the animals living not "happily ever after," but "contentedly to the end of their days."

I had some initial trouble with school readers. I could see Jane run in the pictures. The words seemed redundant and the story lacking in development. Nevertheless, it was novel being able to decipher it for myself. Once I overcame my shyness at reading aloud, and realized most of my classmates weren't used to adult conversation, I had a "breakthrough" in the second half of first grade. By the end of second grade, I began to ransack the wall of books my parents had gotten from the Stalls and the book-of-the-month club.

So, in the hot months of summer—as it turned out, the last summer I was to spend in the Ozarks—I read. I read books about the Ozarks when wolves still ran, about the mythical land of Texas, the Texas of my mind. When I asked which direction Texas lay, my parents pointed south. I assumed it was west and spent the summer with my bearings ninety degrees off. In the Texas of my mind, horses weren't hitched to loads, but only saddled.

In the Ozarks, things were different. The big bay that came to pull logs out of the power-line right-of-way was a draft horse, though the horses I sometimes saw hitched to wagons were probably fox-trotters. I once watched quarter horses, manes clipped in Mohawks and tails tied up, ridden by girls whose jeans I was beginning to notice hugged their legs as tight as their horses hugged the barrels in the barrel race. At the same county fair, a carny from the real Texas sat before the Ferris wheel and batted at the cloud of gnats around his empty eye socket. The horse pulling logs had sores on his legs from the chains. Coloring in first grade, I drew in the sores, but when I read of Silver, I came to believe in places where horses and people were unscarred.

Ralph Moody's stories of his adventures in open-range Colorado were aimed at junior high students. With courage born of ignorance, and plenty of time, I plowed through them. I haven't read them since, so I must have noticed then that the style was inconsistent. The author sometimes injected a boyish ingenuousness meant to appeal to his juvenile readers—"I reckon I got a little hot under the collar"— though in his later autobiographical books, seemingly aimed at an older audience, this was less obvious.

"What thou lovest well remains," says Ezra Pound. "The rest is dross." (Critic Hugh Kenner points out that Pound's father worked in the mint, a source of both this strong imagery and, perhaps, the poet's continuing interest in crackpot economics.) What remained for me is an abiding love for land, a love of strong, utilitarian beauty in horses, people, and books. What remained had to do with puzzling out the meanings of words, spoken, implied, and embodied in the actions of the world around me.

Tribal people (we are told) revere the circle, while people of European tradition love the line, the square, and the box. This is a distinction of convenience, as a moment's reflection will show. Western civilization has been a romance with the wheel from the cart to the chariot to the compass and sextant to the gear to the waterwheel to the main street of any town or suburb where teenagers, despite what community leaders say, worship the circle.

I learned to encircle myself with words as shamans protect themselves with a red line or with chants as circular as the near-palindromic abracadabra, or the rosary. The circle of the forest slowly gave way to the circle of the sky, then to the circle of human faces—the least secure. "Turning and turning in the widening gyre," the falcon does not need the falconer if she only knew it. Again, the margins of my world came clearly drawn, and if I could not represent them graphically, I could say them. The ideal reading light for me is still the blue green submarine light under a tree. Books' links with trees encompass more than the origin of their paper. If one is the entrée into the larger human society of the mind, the other anchors one in the yet larger society of life. Both overreach the individual yet remain immediate, approachable.

Here began my aesthetic, which I call Sylva-poiesis. What we lose when we lose books, letters, and the like to electronic media, become postliterate, as some would have it, are specific connections. These are as elemental to our being as are those our mammal ancestors forged in the forest. The eye, perceiver of space, translates symbols into sounds perceived by the ear and denoting time (think music).

While I was connecting with these sources, however unwittingly, the Scopes "monkey" trial was brewing not far away. All around, the forest was creating tons of life out of thin, thin soil, out of rock and air and sunlight. All I knew about reading was that the light moved, my eyes moved, and I heard and saw things. Sometimes I saw a white horse in moonlight in the Texas of my mind, or heard the young Ralph Moody's grandfather talking to him with a Maine accent. Yet the shifting light was driving the images too, the presence of the trees overhanging. The light was driving water up the trunks of the trees, a small sea of it each hour on each acre of forest, as it drove the words into my head, as strobing lights drive brain waves.

About this time two men died: Ernest Vale and my Grandfather Homer. I can't remember which of the two took me out walking in the clear cold afternoon as my mother was giving birth to my brother in our grandparents' house. Ernest "old man" Vale was our neighbor and my friend in the way old men and young boys often are. He lived with his son Eugene and daughter-in-law Thela in a small house across the road from our property, a quarter mile away through the woods and across one of their fields. Strangely, I do not remember that we talked much, only that he showed me things—how to shuck corn, birds, the hollow log where a fox lived. He asked me not to tell Gene for fear he'd shoot it as a chicken thief.

Gene drove the open Model A truck they used on the farm down into the access road with his chain saw on back, cursing and pulling the crank. He kept a coffee can under the seat so he could piss into it without leaving the truck because the clutch would overheat and grab. It had a name, if memory serves, although it doesn't serve well enough to tell me what the name was. Ernest spent his last year or so confined to bed. The operative word, *invalid*, is especially true where houses are small and the world outside is what validates existence. His bed was in the living room. A mirror perched high in a corner so he could alternate between watching the birds in the yard and the television. I watched my first television show—*Gunsmoke*, in 1958—with him, a disappointment. I was used to listening to it on the radio. The reception was poor, and I could not recognize the snowy pictures. I expected it to be like the stereoscope, three-dimensional. The movement was unconvincing. (I'd seen only a few movies.) The two-dimensional black-and-white figures were like the pictures we imagined in the pine knots on the cabin walls, but less distinct.

Ernest's TB gave him coughing fits. He had little appetite. Gene and Thela washed his plates separately. When he died, I saw Gene and Thela at church services for the first time. I had always assumed they went to another church. They didn't cry. My father explained that some people didn't go to church. Gene said his father was better off.

Everybody cried at my grandfather's funeral, though he was a man unlikely to weep at funerals. I remember my parents telling him of the death of one of his older sons—a man I never met—of a heart attack. Grandfather sat in a kitchen chair and looked old. I was taken out of the room. My father cried openly only when we got to the graveyard.

I stayed with my grandmother the night before the funeral and kept her busy. She cooked her horrible oatmeal, slightly burned as always. She'd lost her sense of smell in her teenage bout with TB, and with it most sense of taste. She couldn't tell the cream had turned bad and poured some on her cereal, but discovered it before she gave me any. She also wanted me close by her the whole time. I even slept with her—the oddest and most frightening part of the experience, since she was normally such a cold, distant, and disapproving presence. Despite the many times she raised her voice, and the rising inflection of annoyance that affected her when she spoke my grandfather's name— Al-FRED!—she wept. It became my job to keep her attention during the funeral. When she saw me watching her she put on a brave front and smiled at me. I began to feel that if I didn't keep her smiling, she would get hysterical. Grandfather looked like the greenhouse flowers surrounding him, pale and powdery.

Grandfather died in Nevada while visiting another of his older sons, the ones from his first marriage my grandmother had been retained to look after. She always seemed to consider their acceptance of her a triumph, her own children something of a disappointment. All had moved away and were successful, one a chiropractor, the others I don't remember. My father looked after her until her death. He had two sisters. They maintained ties to the area.

My grandfather is, in my mind, a composite of the indulgent man I remember and of my mother's stories. When he died I remembered the tickle of his shaving-brush mustache, the blocky blacksmith hands attached to an old man's wrists, his way of teasing my mother. "Got a toothache? Put an ice cube in your mouth and sit on the woodstove." His jokes: "Why don't Christian Scientists have windows in their hospitals? They don't believe in panes." He had a thick English country brogue and left *h* off or put it on seemingly indiscriminately— "Hedward 'as an 'ead ache."

At the funeral parlor in Poplar Bluff, my aunt Barbara Ruth and her fiancé went to a restaurant. Reasonable, they told my father, a

couple of bucks for roast beef, mashed potatoes, vegetable, and i-c-e
c-r-e-a-m. I won points for precociousness, asking my father if I could
have ice cream too, after I finished my dinner. He laughed. I had
defused another potentially sad situation. In the graveyard, red earth
piled to one side, my father's tears dripped off the sides of his nose as
he sat with his head down. "He *was* my father," he said, as if explain-
ing his tears.

I was soon to lose my father to divorce. After a trip with us children
to California to see her family, Mom returned briefly, tried living in
the cabin, couldn't take it, and left. My brother and I returned to
spend another year with him—me eleven, my brother six, my father
forty-two—in St. Louis, north side, the ghetto. Then, letters. Then,
he remarried. I heard later that some of the family shunned him for
marrying a black woman. We stopped corresponding when I was
about fifteen. Later attempts in my twenties brought a few increasingly strained letters, then silence. Screw him, I said. What did I
know? I was twenty-two. I could only imagine what caused his lapses—
his new wife's insecurity? the medication for the epilepsy that could
have killed him at any time in the last—how old is he now? seventy?—
any time in the last fifty years?

The epilepsy. The national epilepsy foundation's symbol is a row of
paper-doll-like figures, the one at the end falling. I was warned by
various adults, by poorly written pamphlets and bad movies, that
anything—drugs, sex, masturbation—could bring it on. I was the
lucky generation it skipped. People still view it with unreasoning awe.
They say the sufferer never sees himself in seizure and so does not
understand the reaction of others. Since the disease, the inherited
kind, at any rate, often comes on at adolescence, the concomitant fear
of social embarrassment is strong. There are dangers, too (though
swallowing one's tongue is not one of them). Falling, for instance. A
blood clot killed a friend I worked with, a man who took drugs, lost
sleep, played loud music, then worked a factory job all day.

This is not a graceful fall, but a dive into deep water with dangerous undertows. Even the less dramatic forms are frightening. A moment's inattention in a pre-industrial world would perhaps be unnoticed, but on the freeway. . . . My daughter's brief adolescent petit mal went unnoticed by everyone until she came of an age to drive and refused, finally confessing her frightening lapses.

The circle of words, the margin that bounded our lives, as well as the threats barely beyond it, expressed itself in a religion that prized eloquence and tried to reach into the commonality of people's lives— a religion continually eroding like the land. The material success that provided the balm for others elsewhere was not to be had. My earlier sense of completeness, a child's carefully constructed cosmology, came apart. My mother and brother and I soon left the land and my father. The loss of place is an agent of the loss of father. The loss of the land— the farm, the neighborhood, the town, the tribe, the wilderness—and estrangement from our fathers have come on apace.

A vivid portrayal of this erasure of the father is William Trow-bridge's "My Father Cannot Draw a Man." Not pastoral by any means, one of the excellences of this elegy is the way it links how we place ourselves in our world and our sense of place:

> On the paper he shoves across the desk
> sprawl three figures, three attempts
> —two, really. One slopes off
> to the left, sprouting a bowler
> from its funhouse head. Beside it
> squirms an eyeless chameleon
> with two tails. The last is a hard
> wavy line.
>
> The doctor studies them,
> jots some notes beneath, clears
> his throat. Trauma, he explains,
> can make the brain lose track
> of the place the body occupies,

of the borders and crosswalks between
where you are and where you're not
till every street leads back
to the same vacant lot. Many
can adjust, he says, but you must watch
such patients. They can wander off,
step out to get the mail and disappear
with hardly a trace.

                    My father and I
watch a man rise from the paper
and wander off toward evening traffic,
outline unsteady, sloping left,
no shoes, baggy slacks, his hat
too large. Lights flow up from the street
before him. My mother stands
at a crosswalk down the block,
where the light blinks "*wait, wait.*"
When he steps off the curb, cars
glide through him. He takes on
their colors, or they take his on.
Hurrying into the rush, he leaves
a hard wavy line.

Electrical storms become living things. They are among the most
complex and volatile processes we study—short of life. Composed of
"cells" clearly visible on computer-enhanced radar, they emit dis-
charges that mimic those at the synapses. Their movements are either
growth or decay; they do not exist in stasis. They are heterogeneous
processes whose character is expressed by both their physical and
their dynamic makeup in time. Being inside one is being swallowed.
They speak to and feed on one another.

An approaching storm is fearsome on the plains. The warning is less in the Ozarks' higher relief. The elevation is not enough to affect the severity of storms or the amount of precipitation in the area. In high mountains, where most human activity confines itself to valleys and lightning rarely strikes within two thousand feet of a house, one has to go looking for storms. On the Ozark Plateau, the sense of threat in the building heat, pressure, and humidity is the same as on the plains, but the sighting time is less. Volleys of thunder come out of an adjoining hollow under a blue sky. When the clouds come, it is likely to be as a dark spiral, a sea-horse head becoming a cross section of a chambered nautilus.

Caught on a canoeing trip as an adult, I felt an old fear. I was high above the streambed, because water can rise as mysteriously as clouds, before or after the storm hits you. Away from the water, far enough from the trees, I wasn't asking for a lightning strike, and even with trees on either side to form a windbreak, I had my tent well pegged down. I was as safe as I could be in the isolated campground. There were no other people around to give or ask advice, but I was confident in my reading of the situation. I was on the south bank of the river, with a ridge between my camp and the most likely path of the storm.

At least I was reasonably sure the ridge was south of me. I had been two days on the Current, which flows south-southeast. But it meanders. I could be facing any direction except due west. From what I remembered of the sun—now too far down to tell, the light diffused by cloud—I was all right. The clouds building up behind the ridge might mean the storm had slipped around me and was moving away. Or they might mean I was facing due south and the draw would funnel the winds directly through the campground.

The storm moved off, showing black and pink curlicues of cloud by last light and roaring through the hollows as it stalked the next county. In the middle of the night sometime (I usually stow my watch and try not to consult it too much), I woke to the round of two whippoorwills, surrounded by a blazing city of fireflies. Far off, like cannon fire on the outskirts of the city, the thunder still went off, and a glow outlined the ridge above, which instantly reversed itself and was outlined against the black sky in firefly light. By morning, the misty river air made a water-color wash of the far bank. Dogwood and redbud softly highlighted a tangle of green and gray branches against the granite wall.

Not all storms are so benign. Some came much closer. My father was out in a thunderstorm, putting the chickens into the chicken coop so they wouldn't panic and hurt themselves flying into the high wire of their pen. A lightning bolt and thunder crack came together.

I was seven or eight. I feared my parents' fights meant I would be separated from my father. The flash lit up the coop. I almost remember the chicken wire glowing. I saw my father closing the gate before the darkness of the storm closed in again. I was sure he had been hit.

After the storm, we walked the woods perhaps three hundred yards in the opposite direction from the chicken coop. The bolt had hit an oak and spiraled from the high fork, down several limbs, to a point near the ground, where it left the tree for earth. The exploding steam in the wood had blown twenty-foot splinters fifty yards uphill. My father was nowhere near it.

The storms worried us and entertained us. Walking down through a neighbor's cornfield from the house of the ocean room, we heard a loud crack. Soon a whirring sound came past us and the corn above our heads rattled and split, tassels and leaves breaking and dropping all around us. My parents began to shout. From the farmhouse up near the road came the neighbor's voice, calling my parents' names. We went up and met him and his wife, and had several pleasant visits after that. He never fired a warning shot a foot over our heads again. I thought of the warnings on the boxes of .22 rifle shells: "Lethal at distances up to one mile." We were more careful about telling him we'd be walking on his property. People were fond of our neighbor's sweet corn, as we were. We never had to steal any but were always asked over to eat it with him and his wife. They both extolled the cobs' virtues as toilet paper. I don't remember trying it.

Before I learned the escape of reading, the days my parents called good corn-growing days were a torment. Incipient thunder boomed in my pulse all afternoon as the heat and humidity rose and the pressure of distant thunderheads mashed the air to the ground. Dust fell on every surface like a mist making way for the air to grow even more water-saturated. Rivulets of sweat marked trails down my round boy's belly through the grime. Years later I was to hear on the St. Louis radio the death count during summers like these, for the old truly cannot bear the worst of this heat in the river valleys. Surely then it was my imagination that not only the bug bites I habitually courted, not only the galling lines of the sweat rivers, but my whole body itched, crawling with static that made the very dust move on my skin.

Walking down to our vegetable patch one day in the heat I felt physical shock and heard a foreign noise, then a scream—light, trains, cats, and steam and maybe my mother calling my father's name and me screaming. Surely I saw the paw or the tail come out of some invisible place and slap the ground like the angel of light's hoof. The sun was shining and a bolt of lightning (for I soon recognized that's what it was) had shot up out of the ground into the sky. Not fork lightning. Not St. Elmo's fire, or the lightning balls that travel fence posts or roof beams. Not the ball of fire that traveled the spine of my grandparents' house and knocked the chimney cockeyed. This was a bolt of pure zigzag, shooting up and quivering like a blade in the ground before being sucked up or in or back to wherever such things go.

This was seizure, this rapture, this the tongue of flame the Pentecostalists speak of. This was the glossolalia my father spoke when in the arms of whatever power made him strange to other men. At the time, of course, I stood with my parents, a shocked child. Lightning burned certain images into my mind, and to these, later, accrued words and, in the words, memory. So I remember certain places and incidents lit by a strange nervous light, like lightning at night.

The path to our cabin ran from the road through the Vales' field, past the hollow log where the fox hid, down the ravine where my play camp was, and up the other side. It was so familiar, we could follow it home in the dark, even by starlight. One night, carrying our month's supplies in the dark of a storm, we had to make it by lightning flash. Each flash burned the scene into our retinas, an unfamiliar landscape in black and silver, like a solarized photograph manipulated in the bath. It was a collage in time. Each flash was really many flashes, a flickering followed by its sound, which made the eye flinch and the burned-in image waver again. The seeing and the hearing—the map of footfall and feel—blow away in the wind and the sound. We go primitive, finding our way through the forest again after generations on the plains, again marginal, living on the edge of our senses.

The image burned into the eye is hard to correct. The brain knows you are moving, recognizes landmarks and can guess the paces to the next tree. That pesky image stays floating ahead of you like a museum diorama. Brushing your face will not clear the scene. The next lightning flash lasts just long enough for the eye to lay a new image over the old; it's not long enough to recognize in the negative image of the tree trunks, now bright with rain, a familiar landmark.

So much for foresight, for plans. May as well close your eyes and plunge ahead. If the landscape is truer in the mind, and if it lives better there with words to keep it company, then I have my father with me always, not only in this electrical storm that is my truest being, this process that remains the same no matter how many cells I slough off, or how many new flickering images the world overlays. The storms I stand in are only word storms. Yet they strike as deep into the earth. They arrive with as much warning or as little, and they shed their shuddering light on a landscape I have learned to trust.

"An electrical storm in the brain" is how epilepsy is sometimes described, and the process is about as unpredictable and complex. The zigzags of electroencephalograms show irregularities. Starting in some localized area, these travel by neural pathways in some kind of bleed-through (induction) to neighboring parts or to regions not obviously connected. In the fifties, when my father's hyper-religious neighbors misunderstood his condition, even the most sophisticated researchers still believed in something called the "epileptic personality."

Some researchers considered this personality so pronounced—characterized by a "sticky affectivity," which supposedly made the epileptic either "emotionally impoverished" or "hypersensitive"—they believed they could identify epileptics by personality tests. This "stickiness," this "glischroid" or "viscous" quality, supposedly rendered the affected person tiresomely verbose on trivial details—the type who would wander wide in telling a story, but return repeatedly, stubbornly to their agenda in conversation. Sometimes linked with a morphological "type," epileptics were compared in one report to Dostoyevsky's characters—the dull, civil servant types. The writers, French psychoanalysts, didn't say how Dostoyevsky (an epileptic, as were Alexander the Great, Julius Caesar, William Pitt, Byron, Handel, and possibly Buddha and Muhammad) found the objectivity to draw such portraits, or whether they found his prose "sticky" or circular. Later, psychologists suggested many other sources of "typical" epileptic behavior—societal pressures, the hormonal shocks of adolescence, the long-term effects of the barbiturates given as anticonvulsants.

As I write these words, I experience a bit of the danger of amateur diagnosis. When I reread drafts of my prose, do I detect a mechanical harping, an insistent returning to trivial points? Am I, carrying as I do an as-yet-unidentified gene that gives me and my descendants a predilection to seizures, "sticky?" If anyone in the family has a reputation for long-windedness, it's me, whom my aunts called "Professor Homer" since childhood. Certainly my father, who decided to move on with his life and ceased making any claims, became increasingly distant, wasn't displaying clinging behavior. Such lay analysis, like New Age pseudo-mysticism, is hard to avoid.

Recently, the fashionable therapies for all sorts of ailments have included the power of visualization, meditation, crystal therapy, and generally "getting in touch with yourself and nature." In a sense I believe it all, but feel an old sore spot open when the tenor of the conversation turns that hard-to-define corner between good advice and moral censure—the "all disease is bad karma / you must be carrying some tension / clean up your act / you should have thought of that" response to illness. The New Age response sounds strangely like fundamentalist guilt at times and can carry a primitive element of pack fear of the sick individual. This from people who can afford the extravagance of high-fiber diet aids while still there are folks eating clay to keep hunger away. A former housemate of mine can afford to believe that sitting colored glass on top of water glasses will "charge" the water with color when sun shines through the glass and the water, the proper dose for the day determined by dangling a crystal over the various glasses and observing the response. As Flannery O'Connor's Bible salesman says, "You ain't so smart. I been believing in nothing [or everything] for a long time." Or Roethke, who believed self-dissection to be "a virtue when / it operates in other men."

So don't judge my parents' neighbors too harshly. Don't you dare. Prayer, faith, patience, Dilantin, a mixture of apple cider vinegar and honey, an entirely homegrown diet, Phenobarbital—none of that cured my father's grand mal. Prayer didn't work on the hydrocephalic boy whose parents decided to stop treatment and rely on God. The preacher's daughter, Suzy, almost died from the effects of the early polio vaccine. If it wasn't prayer that saved her, it wasn't science. On the other hand, there was my Grandmother Homer, as puritanical and intolerant a person as I've ever met, healthy as a horse after that childhood bout with TB. Religion and science come out a draw.

I've always thought if there was any imbalance in Father's life, it was in pure tight-assed, stoic rectitude. Maybe he needed a time of dissolution. Having let go of him in life, I dread the letter or phone call that will tell me of his death. I fear his meekness, would rather imagine him charging with Li Po into the river to possess the moon.

The Drownt Boy

And miles to go before I sleep

THE LIFE JACKET FEELS LIKE A PANICKED SWIMMER clutching at my back. The water is dark under the heavy foliage. I try to kick up, but I feel disoriented. Somehow I'm being turned. It is very cold. My arms feel heavy. The underarm straps pull up against my armpits. I open my eyes but can't see anything but a diffuse green light. I relax and let the jacket pull me up.

On the surface, I float easily. Either I imagined the twisting undertow, or I'm out of it. There's no canoe and no Reese. I'm afraid he's been pulled into the chute for an instant before I realize there's no chute. I'm facing upriver. I twisted around in the eddy. Reese is scrambling to stay on top of the canoe, and we both laugh as it rolls over. Our teeth chatter. He still has his paddle. We are in still, deep water, past the submerged snag, but well above the beginning of the chute. I start to kick toward the shallow side of the pool, trying to drag the canoe. I burble for Reese to head for shore. My hand slips and I float off. Suddenly, I feel Reese's arm under my chin, and I almost panic. It feels as if he's slipped off the canoe and is grabbing me for support. I'm not sure I'm a strong enough swimmer to pull us both in.

"You okay?"

Reese is still holding onto the canoe. He's a big, strong kid. He has seen me flailing around and burbling and is trying to pull me back. This time I catch my breath before trying to talk.

We are soon able to touch bottom and guide the inverted canoe. Completely filled with water, it is hard to move. Reese suggests we let it float into a root wad. I am adamant if not articulate:

"No root wads. No root wads."

So we pull and push across the river to a sandy, narrow bank where we jam the canoe among some roots. My paddle is still floating in the eddy, and the five-gallon bucket is loose and bumping along toward the chute, despite the six-hundred-pound-test parachute chord. I shudder a bit slipping into the water again. The river gave me a gentle but unmistakable nudge. I might have imagined the twisting pull of the cold water. Maybe I flailed around and got myself turned backward in the river, but it took a strong eddy or side current to push the canoe into the limb. It's a thang there.

Soon I have our gear up on the bank. In all, maybe five minutes have passed since I said we were okay. We strain at the canoe but can't roll it over to dump the water. We have to pull it back into deeper water, roll and lift it. On the bank, we shiver in the light breeze. Everything is soaked. We took out the camera to take pictures of the vultures perched on fog-shrouded snags over our heads. I didn't get the lid completely sealed on the bucket. Our lunch, miraculously, is only damp. When I hold up Reese's camera, a stream of water trickles out of it.

We wring out our shirts, and our formerly dry clothes, wring out the towels, and hang everything on branches. I look hard to make sure we're not sitting on or draping our clothes over poison ivy, determined not to make matters worse by overlooking any obvious hazards.

Shivering in our shorts, our clothes drying as well as they might, we eat lunch. The river bag is dry. I had lashed the bucket's bail—its curved wire handle—to the crossbar of the canoe. The bail has been ripped from the bucket and is nowhere to be found. The water container fared better, but I'm not sure river water hasn't seeped in. There are no facilities between us and Akers, our destination, so it will have to serve. The diffuse sunlight is probably burning us, but it does not warm us. Soon we must get back in the river.

Reese is in no hurry. He suggests portaging around the esses below us, across about a quarter mile of gravel bar. I point out that we went over in a pool. Riffles haven't given us any trouble. Besides, if we avoid every danger on the river, we'll have to portage all the way back to camp.

"Why not? It's better than going over in the river again."

"It's probably fifteen miles."

"Maybe we could leave the canoe and walk back."

It's time to get going before we lose our nerve. If Reese's confidence in my canoe handling is shaken, mine is not much better. Under the water, I felt its claim on me: my baptism in a tributary of this river, my near drowning in Logan Creek, the bright dime of water at the bottom of the well my grandfather dug. This water comes from the ridges near our old place, near my grandparents' graves. "He was an hundred and ten and his waters were not diminished." Who was that? Abraham? Methuselah?

We take off, paddling hard to get back in the current, shoot past the root wads, look down into the pools gouged out around them. The river does not get better. A sleeping bag hangs from a tree above the waterline. Farther down, a tent filled with water hangs like a blue testicle from a branch. In one long chute, Reese holds onto the gunwales and shivers. Yesterday, he would have hooted and jumped up and down to make waves. "I'm shivering and I'm not even cold," he says, though his lips are blue.

We have to navigate more downed trees, mostly sycamore, the leaves fragrant, the water roaring through the upper branches. We shoot across the drowned boles with no sense of victory. Fear makes us efficient. We are shooting the flood like pros, grim. I ask Reese why he no longer goads me to take the fastest water.

"That was before we went over."

I feel much the same. Who do I think I am? Daniel Boone? Meriwether Lewis? Why should I be angry with the concessionaires for not saving me from my own stupidity? If a guy from Nebraska wants to float the flooded river on a cloudy day, what's it to them? They told us to wear our life jackets. If we don't panic, we won't drown. If we pulled out and sat on the bank, the rangers would come looking for us before dark. It's only as dangerous as we make it.

Often we're right on top of downed trees before we can see the openings. My bruised palms and scraped chest are more noticeable as circulation returns. We are passing a large sandbar with many downed sycamores when I see we are being pulled into yet another river-bridging trunk. This time there is no gap between the leafy limbs at the crown. Fifty feet from the trunk, we sweep across a gravel bar, and I jump out and plant my feet to stop us. Reese, in the bow, gets a close view of the boughs before I manage to pull the canoe out of the current.

While Reese stretches his legs, I empty the sharp gravel out of my river shoes and consider the topography. We are standing on a sandbar that has succeeded the underlying gravel—another sign the river is reestablishing the sandbars of centuries past. I am almost glad we came.

We have to portage fifty yards across the sandbar and lift the canoe over two downed trees. The circulation and feeling return to our lower bodies with exercise. My feet are soggy with three hours of constant immersion in wet canvas shoes. Reese has newer and seemingly better synthetic river shoes. I walk the sandbar barefoot to dry out my feet, and rinse out my shoes before putting them on. My first steps in placing the canoe back in the river refill them with sand. Dry, it looked fine as talc. In my shoes it feels like pea gravel.

I am dipping my feet in the water, then angling my leg out the side so the water and, I hope, the sand will dribble out my hightops past my raw ankles, when I hear a johnboat coming upriver. I am careful to look for snags before edging toward the bank. Still, we drift to the end of the pool and into an easy series of riffles without seeing the boat. I can hear the engine intermittently.

We see the two rangers standing in their johnboat far off. One is holding the boat steady against some saplings as the other reaches into the branches of a tree for something. Before we get into hailing distance the man in the bow has climbed out and is working his way across a wet and swampy-looking bank in search of valuables. He's found someone's handmade quilt and is trying to unwrap its sodden folds from a tree.

The ranger in the stern is sitting as we approach and asks us about conditions upriver. I tell him about the tree across the stream, and he mentions another only two bends farther along. "There's a spill of water over it deep enough to float you. If you hit it straight, you should be okay."

Then we are past them, and there is no time for further questions.

Being canoe-bound for hours at a time is a telling experience. Reese and I handle the enforced intimacy well. We're not ready to kill each other. We are both rigid, straining to see forward. This makes the canoe handle stiffly. Two more bends pass with no sign of the tree.

We hear it first. A single tree such as the maple in front of us makes a noise like a waterfall—a sound much more intimidating than its actual threat. The water is glassy smooth above it. We cannot see the opening in the green wall of leaves, but we can see where it must be. The windy whisper surges over us like an aerosol of sound. We angle for the break between two boughs and find the trough, leading across a surprising and off-angled drop. We turn by habit, and are over so easily it is almost a disappointment.

Soon we are in a spreading pool that promises to become even wider beyond its sandbar. We put in and cross the bar, being careful not to walk through the reedy low spots where snakes could lie con-

cealed. Water moccasins, pygmy rattlers, timber rattlers, copperheads—
all can swim if they have to. Floods wash them out of their bushes,
out of the grass and leaf piles where they hunt, and out of the slack-
water sloughs with their harvest of frogs. We aren't immune from
disaster, though perhaps the local snake handlers would quote Luke,
chapter 10, verse 19, where "saints tread on snakes and scorpions," or
Mark 16:18 about "taking up serpents."

A church built not on rock but on sandbars. So things develop here
in isolation—a deep pool where the sandbar traps water from a small
feeder stream. In such tanning pools, people would rinse their hides,
after curing them in tannic acid derived from the nearby oaks. Across
the pool from us an old couple is fishing. The man waves and I ask
how far to Cedargrove. Just around the curve. We can almost see the
low-water bridge from here.

In the calm water above the bridge, the green wall of the forest
reflects. We are a sliding image among snags piercing the surface,
miniature headlands obscuring the inlets behind. A red gash in the
bank bears the road down on a ribbon of clay. We make for the end of
the bridge where the water is shallow. A trickle overruns the roadway
and six vortices dimple the surface. We must cross the bridge and
portage the canoe across a gravel embankment. One lane is flooded
all the way across, so we float the canoe past the sucking whirlpools.
Again, several culverts jammed with debris knock and rattle as the air
and water yodel a desperate keening around them.

The cedars of Cedargrove are long gone. In the rushing chute
below the bridge several men and boys fish the afternoon away. We
walk down a raw side channel, dry now the initial flood is past, not to
disturb them. We return for our supplies—the heavy bucket of wet
clothes and the paddles. We put in at a backwater, and it takes a bit of
paddling to get into the current again. Two-foot waves break over
deeply submerged boulders. It is easy canoeing in the center.

The current is twisted rope. We weave between individual strands.
Detritus of the flood washes up beside us and sinks again—leaves,

branches, pinecones. Everything here bears the whorled mark of the vortex. The stripped snags spiral their grain up. Our femurs, twisted bones in our sore legs, have grown this way since we twisted at the ends of our umbilical cords. The spiral is the map of organic form, always indirection, never a straight line, but also not truly a circle. The river is extorting this line of thought from me (*extort:* literally "to twist out of"). We just passed the halfway point and I'm wrung out. My shoulders knot—another spiral set up in my flesh, a propensity I have no doubt inherited through the helix of the genes.

Fortunately, the last half of our run looks faster and easier than the first. It took over four hours to make the bridge. Soon we see the wave of water shooting across the channel at Welch Spring, far downriver. This is the one problem we were warned about. We put up against a tree where a steep eroded bank runs up to flatwoods above. We can see how the wave that seemed to block the entire river actually shunts into a calm pool. Downstream, a fallen tree leans upside down, its roots on the high bank, crown in the river. We will have to canoe under it into a long rough chute. Not too difficult unless we get turned sideways going in.

When I say we'll be fine, Reese says, "That's the last thing I heard before we went over." Healthy, I think. Teasing me is better for him than sitting in the front of the canoe and shaking.

"Reese! Look up!" I say halfway down the chute.

Twenty feet above us, camper trailers hang in the treetops. Out of their open doors swing bedding and paneling and cabinetwork with drawers dangling by their metal gliders—accordions unfolded into the air. The narrow chute between these cliffs must have squeezed an extra ten feet out of the flood.

Farther down, the river widens without slowing. Another facet of the hills opens. First on one side and then on the other, limestone cliffs edge the river. The scalloped hills above layer bend after bend. We are probably about an hour from Akers and the end of our labors. Now we expect the campground in a couple of looks.

A look as a measure of distance is, like the term *flatwoods,* a self-evident local expression. Here, where roads and rivers slalom around ridges, the measure is as accurate as it is subjective. It is a constant of the human scale that one wants to know when one can see the destination of a trip.

Of course, the actual landing is a good half-dozen looks further than I expect it. We begin to dawdle. Reese manages to splash me with a wild stroke, and I flick water off my paddle back at him. Soon we are both wet. We'd work harder at it if it were warm—might even risk dumping the canoe on a warm day with a clear river under us. It is cloudy to the west, bringing on false dusk in midafternoon. Rising breeze nips at our soaked torsos.

A gap in the trees ahead. A long stretch of slack water on the inside of a bend. The campground sign slides from the screen of riverside shrubs. Below I see the cable across the river where the ferry essays the current. With a final ceremony of splashing, we hook back toward the gravel bar where we put in two days ago. I cast a hopeful eye for my binocular case. No luck. Who was that Greek philosopher—the can't-put-your-feet-in-the-same-river-twice guy? Heraclitus?

Along the route we decided we've earned a steak dinner in town tonight. We put our equipment in what order we can, pack everything we won't be using, hang our soaked clothes on a length of parachute cord, and head for the hot showers at the big campground down the road.

Our cheeks are red with windburn and blood flow. The family restaurant, complete with salad bar, occupies the first floor of what was once the Eminence Hotel, later a newspaper office, then several other businesses according to the historical gloss on the back of the menu. Hominy and local slaw in the salad bar, the owners named on the menu, two tables constantly full of locals congenial to outsiders.

One young woman, perhaps an owner, waits tables and runs the cash register. Rain has put a big dent in business. I go for the pork-chop dinner, ignoring my mother's injunction, literally hardening my heart. I listen in on the banter between a table of women and the slightly younger waitress they tease mercilessly. I catch only references to the woman's husband, and the occasional rejoinder about having to put up with this for three more months. She doesn't look pregnant. The women remind me of my recent researches into local herb lore. Chamomile, tansy, cedarberry . . . pennyroyal and snakeroot for abortifacients (the Greeks used henna and plumbago, or leadwort). Turpentine for female complaint. Isn't there something about teasing a pregnant woman? A sort of shivaree?

" . . . one or two a year comes up missing," a man at the table against the wall is saying, "ever one within one or two hundred yards of where they went in." The searchers have not found the drownt boy. It's five o'clock Thursday, six days since the drowning, seven hours since we tipped in the river.

Pork chops and applesauce balanced on my fork, I rethink our spill, the sudden power of the eddy in the still pool, the little tug at my feet. I inwardly congratulate us both for handling the river so well—despite my questionable wisdom in canoeing the flood in the first place.

Reese takes his steak bone in a bag for the scrawny whippet, 103, and we set off for our last campfire. On the way down the now familiar Highway 19 north to our campground, we cross the Jacks Fork. It is flooded and closed to canoes. Farther along the road, two cars have been winched from the river below the bridge at Sinking Creek. Large American cars, they must have been on the gravel bar, a popular camping and fishing spot locally. Gray silt covers both. Streaks of color show through where the workers leaned against them. They swiped at the windows to see inside. One looks as though the campers had time to throw all their bedding and some camp gear inside, but then had to abandon the car.

Before we drive down from the ridge road to return to our campground, I turn down an unused track and we get out to stroll through the open forest. Unlike the river forest, the undergrowth here is thin, the canopy sparse. On the dry ridge, black oak, shagbark, and occasional pine dominate the forest. There is plenty of light for the understory, but little water. Shrubs tap deep for underground sources. I pick witch hazel and sassafras. While I'm gathering, Reese explores along the track, finds no clue to its destination, probably an abandoned homestead along the river. Artifacts almost evenly cover the forest floor: rusting bedsprings; old stove legs and vague metal lumps; a bottle, the mildewed cork still in, the label a mere stain on the wavery glass walls.

Back at camp, while Reese searches for 103, I empty the trunk of boughs and bag the leaves. We've also been carrying a fair load of wood around—remnants of a couple of bundles we bought last night and kept dry in the trunk. I am profligate with stove fuel, and we have an ax to split lots of kindling. The fire starts easily, but its heat falters when mist drifts in with sunset.

River fog reaches just over our heads. The moon has been up for an hour or so and is bright on the mist, on the grass and the standing water. From the dark mass of riverside trees, the peeled upper branches of sycamores and cottonwoods blanch. The trees on the slopes absorb the moonlight completely. One dead snag glows in the dark body of the hill across from us. To the northwest, moonlight touches on clouds.

I build up the fire, and we take turns staring through the fog, across the open grass of the campground for 103. We place the bone in the grass—far enough away not to scare her and close enough to keep the pack from it. When the moon has climbed high above us, we see her white hide and raw numbers at the edge of the open area. She will not come closer.

Later, the thunder and lightning approach again, and soon it begins to sprinkle. We strike the tent and pack up before the rain starts in earnest and spend the night in the car, a worse mistake than any I made on the river. I should either have stuck it out in the tent and taken the chance of having to pack up in the rain or driven to Salem and searched out a motel. What sleep we manage is cramped. I wake groggy, facing eight road hours with a sore back and stiff legs, hoping a good breakfast will improve both our tempers.

Bacon and eggs go a long way toward equipoise. The bacon is thick, could be local. I like to imagine pigs foraging acorns on the local farms. The wild and half-wild pigs are much less common since open range is gone. Back here at the restaurant of the pregnant woman, an older woman waits tables. The man who talked of the drowning is back at his table with his sister-in-law, her grown daughter, and a friend. They are talking about the rain and the chance of more floods when I interrupt them to ask about the search.

"Found him in that pool below the campground," the man answers. "Right alongside the island."

Precisely where the night search was going on night before last. It was late yesterday afternoon before they found him, while we were in town. We didn't talk to anybody after dinner.

"Hung up in a root wad." He doesn't seem interested in further conversation. The women have been sitting silently. I go back to my breakfast.

Their talk turns to river running and people who don't have any business there. I should feel chastened. I'm sore and chapped from wind and water, gravel and branch. Reese has chapped cheeks burned into his tan. We both grin and pack away the food. Reese asks why I didn't mention dumping us in the river. They never asked. We're feeling better than necessary, and I hope it lasts the drive home, the long day I can feel accreting behind my eyelids.

We've "made the riffle," and finish our breakfast listening to our neighbors talk about those who didn't, or their own experiences. Sister-in-law says they capsized at the head of a well-known chute. She was bruised all over by the time they reached the bottom.

En route to Ellington, we stop at a Park Service visitor center. It's closed, as are the blacksmith, johnboat maker, quilter, whiskey stiller, demonstrating their crafts at scattered park sites. In the old field next to the hundred-yard-wide river, a big whitetail buck whips through the dried weed stalks at better than our twenty-five miles an hour. His coat is red, very dark. He is beyond a fence overgrown with brush. I watch him through the gaps.

Ellington still has diagonal parking in the middle of Main, a broad, frontier-town look to the storefronts, the few *belles maisons* in disrepair.

"What happened here?"

"Nothing I know of," I respond, thinking Reese is getting so desperate for entertainment that he's actually come to enjoy my narratives on historical sites. I wonder what he imagines. "You mean like gunfights?"

"No. I mean the town. What happened to it? It looks beat up?"

This is far away from picturesque parkside cabins, vacation homes, and the occasional small farmhouse or double-wide. Old houses are neither preserved nor left to decay in painterly dignity as are the riverside homesteads. Here, a trailer grafted onto a house and painted to match has peeled and settled at a different rate than the house. A circle of tin patches the resulting crack in the roof. The old supermarket and drugstore, still bearing names of my childhood classmates, stay open in the face of larger chain stores out on the highway. Everything is just noticeably further given to decay than in other Midwest small towns.

On the tram road heading north over former railroad right-of-way, white frame houses balance on their four concrete footings. Hogs root acorns in bare earth around a small stand of blackjack. The swale between the trees has become a wallow. Tin roofs flash in hazy light, and the red gravel in the asphalt glows sullenly where passing wheels have pressed the tar out. A beat-up town, and out of town is worse.

After passing the first rises, running along the creekside for a mile, past the old horse ranch and through a shady cut, the road climbs steadily straight to the ridges. The logging train's limited power dictated cuts through minor hillocks, then a straight run across the level ridge. Red bites open in the iron-rich soil. Mined out. Splintered houses center sudden openings in the forest. The asphalt runs farther than last time I was here, seven miles, before changing to red gravel. Then, section markers and private roads where D-9 tracks collect water.

Past a long straight run, I come to a deadening of girdled oaks with twenty-year-old pines rising out of it. The Vale place, house smaller and closer to the road than I remember it, barn down for decades, sweet-corn patch and grazing field deep in sumac. Across the road, the power lines dip vertiginously down a gulch and up the other side. Our old cabin site. I pull into the cutout, and we walk up under the power lines into the unfenced meadow. On the slight rise a quarter mile away I can see the yard and a corner of the new house built there, size and shape unclear in the haze. Dew drenches the knee-high grass and soapweed. Our pants cling to our legs.

From here, the trail led through the woods to our cabin. As a child, I navigated it daily. The hollow log old man Vale claimed housed the local fox is long since rotted into the ground. Probably a gray fox, making up for its lack of colorful coat with agility, running across downed logs and climbing trees at need. Squirrels, foxes, woodpeckers, all make enviable homes in trees and downed logs. As a child, I could imagine nothing finer than a home in a large hollow tree. I am staring down the well of reminiscence, the child tumbled in the baptismal waters of the local creek staring back in reflection.

We drive to the lane leading to the cabin site. A steel stock gate, chained and padlocked, shuts it off. There is a grazing field beyond, then woods, then the gully with sinkholes, then thicker woods, the turnaround outside the yard. Oh, yes . . . wandering like a tedious argument of insidious intent along the side field where a heifer bel-

lowed through hot nights with a painful udder after losing her calf—
separating the field from the orchard whose trees' heavy limbs were
even then arcs coiled groundward with the stringy bark ratcheting
out along the recurve, apple, pear—there, protecting all but the widest
spread of fruit limb from the grazing cows and rooting pigs throughout years of open range, ran the zigzag fence, its split rails of god-
knew-what wood grayed beyond recognition in the heat and wet and
cold, silver in moonlight as we walked back from my grandparents',
dull gray in midsummer, and in spring rain developing sudden blooms
of green moss.

Across from the fence would lie the blackberry patch, walkwayed
with pine slabs. And from there and there, all padlocked behind the
steel gate hung on L hooks screwed in the ironwood gatepost. . . . Or
there were once these things. I don't want to brave dogs and shotguns to climb over. The open range closed long ago.

We climb back in the car to leave. As soon as we start to move the
fox lopes across the road. I stop. He poses on top of a log in sunlight,
showing off the red ruff below the gray saddle giving him his name.
He turns and ambles into the moving shadows. A flash of white, his
tail finally disappears.

I do not recognize the name on the mailbox at my grandparents'
place. The original house is a scattering of stones. Even the chimney
has fallen now. The stock pond is nearly silted in. A low long house
gone early into middle age replaces the small frame house that was
here a few years ago. Along the fence, a selection of wrecked cars. It's
far from clear whether anyone lives here.

Past the collapsed Corridon Union Church sits Grogan's store, gas
pumps standing dull red, the little glass bubbles empty of gas since
before Reese or my daughter was born. I think what they'd be worth
in an antique store in Omaha. Inside the store, the oiled floor is still
solid, the empty shelves in place. The board porch separates from the
building, slanting into the gravel, steps gone. Here old men sat.
Inside women picked up mail handed through the grille from the

wooden post office cubbyholes in the next room. The wives talked of the propriety of the Johnson family bringing guitars to church. My mother played piano and disapproved. The men out front were likely discussing technique.

After taking two wrong turns, I find the graveyard. A note on the gate announces donations needed for upkeep will be collected at the grocery store down the road. I have a vague memory of my grandparents' gravestone, but it takes a few minutes to find it even in this small plot—surprising how many are here. Not my father, I find, though he could be; I haven't had news of him for five years. Alfred and Auroa (a variant of Aurora) Homer (a name from the western Midlands of England for one who makes helmets). Strange it never occurred to me that both my wife's and my names also begin with A. The site is well tended. Perhaps Aunt Sarah Lois . . . or have others of the family moved back? Retired? We put our dead to rest, also those places inside us that die of old age. We find peace. Burn the heart of a murdered man. Sprinkle cornmeal over the corpse, lay corn on the grave.

We pass the small grocery taking donations. I drive past, though I have to stop within a mile for both of us to visit the bushes down a Forest Service turnout. Donations to the groundwater accepted here. This is now the Mark Twain National Forest. The day is turning hot and quiet. Back among sparse undergrowth, the light and shade shift as a light breeze shakes the leaves. Here, too, the forest floor is stippled with old bottles, bits of indeterminate metal.

I see a perfect patent medicine bottle, then, in the wheel ruts, a blue-bellied lizard. The two blue things, pale lizard belly and dark glass, look cool and I long to touch them. The bottle would join a growing pile of such acquisitions—goat hair plucked from bushes of the Olympics, turkey feather, orbicular jasper, seashells. . . . I don't want souvenirs. I call for Reese. If we make good time, we can reach Jefferson City before lunch.

I have hardened my heart.

The Meek

Nothing in the world
is softer and weaker than water.
Yet for attacking the hard and strong
you'll find nothing to outdo it,
and nothing that can even replace it.

If water defeats the unyielding,
the weak can defeat the strong—
everyone says so. It's become a cliché.
Yet who can tell us how it is done?

This is why the sage says: "Be the water
that takes on the filth of the state; only then
can you be lord of the altars of earth and grain.
Take upon yourself the evil of the government
    this is being king of the world."

The truth often seems its reverse.

Lao Tzu, *Tao Te Ching*

ONLY ONCE OR TWICE WERE MY BROTHER AND I HUNGRY—
and then only after my parents had been living on short rations

awhile. My more immediate concern was fitting in at school. The homemade bread my mother baked in the woodstove was unlike the foamy, white squares town kids ate, after they carefully peeled off the crusts and threw them away. Some foods bore repetition better than others. Pinto beans and cornbread were staples. A week of pears and green beans not only produced near-debilitating diarrhea but left me with a gag reflex at the smell of pears.

As several friends have noted, another lasting effect of the experience is that I don't take their struggles with diet very seriously. Since your diet consists of whatever you eat, it seems hard to be "off" one unless you stop eating. I'm accused of lacking empathy. A friend once argued, sincerely, that he shouldn't be expected to take the same responsibility for his actions as I because he was deprived; having never been poor, he'd never had the opportunity to learn self-discipline.

In having been hungry—never for long, never to the point of permanent damage—and having seen my parents worry and argue about where the actual next meal was coming from, I share more with people my parents' age than with my pampered generation. In the thirties, President Hoover stated flatly that no one was starving in the United States. On a hunting trip to the Appalachians, locals insisted he accompany them to a cabin where a child lay dead from starvation. Thinking back on our neighbors, I recognize the signs of poverty—retardation, blindness, missing teeth—problems treatable with prevention, diet, and education. Though there is strength in the rural poor folks who face privation and survive, it is a rangy strength. The strong-jawed Li'l Abners and buxom Daisy Maes are only in cartoons.

After a bad winter exacerbated by the spoiling of some of our canned goods, my parents went into food growing more seriously. The first step is to buy, borrow, or barter for a mule and a double shovel. We had the plow and arranged the loan of the mule. With these two weapons, poverty is on the run. Several types of eating disorders, depression, ennui, and other symptoms of what I'd call spiritual poverty could be helped with these tools. As the ecologist Paul Shepard says, we need to reinitiate the dialogue with nature from which we learned so much. The mule, I suggest, would be a good place to start, like the pets that often bring catatonic children out of themselves. For the mule, poor sterile sport of nature and in some ways a perfect example of man's tampering, is in other ways less domesticated than either the horse or the shuffling ox. This is the mule's legacy from its father, the ass. Not obedient, though loyal, not so much stubborn as aware of its own limits, a mule won't hurt itself as a horse will, trying to pull too heavy a load too far.

The mule we borrowed was a tall, dark animal, probably part Percheron—even-tempered as mules go. He wouldn't pull on command, but zinging his ears with dirt clods got him moving, and he kept moving until stopped. Then he needed more dirt clods. My father let me drive him for one row. I dangled from the plow handles, the reins looped over my shoulders.

On one of his fruitless monthly visits, the local Jehovah's Witness pulled up the generous cuffs of his blue suit pants to show the marks of years of mule skinning. The fundamentalist white shins were pitted and scored with marks of blows that remained blue as bruises. Some would claim this was because he trained mules for sale and didn't develop a relationship of trust with them. An old farmer near Ellington who used mules for transportation, hauling, and plowing trusted them more than people. The blue scars were a testament to the mule's intelligence. While a horse will kick wildly in panic, hurting itself in the traces, a mule aims. Mules, like most traction animals, must be used often enough to be worth year-round feeding. We never bought one, opting for a rototiller when a windfall came our way. I would have liked a horse, but they eat more than they're worth. A mule makes better sense for the Ozarks. Still, I can see why the poor Jehovah's Witness felt a calling to "witness for the Lord."

The double shovel, like the letterset printing press, the treadle sewing machine, and the screen door, is an example of benign technology. It needs no improvement. Though this light plow will not break heavy sod, it will likewise not dig too deep. Unlike the heavier moldboard plow, it does not lead to as much soil compaction at the plow sole, or bottom reach of the blade. It's a match for the light, small-footed mule, which is also less likely to add to compaction and erosion than a horse. The mule survives on a higher roughage diet than a horse—almost as high a fiber count as a health club client— and produces fertilizer out of it. In turn, the double shovel is perfect for mixing in the compost and fertilizer such poor land needs.

We kept a compost pile. That was all we used, since the area was large and level, and we weren't using it for high-intensity farming. We had enough space to rotate crops as well. About an acre (give or take, making allowances for a child's judgment, my memory after thirty years) produced a great deal. Enhanced by several abandoned fruit orchards and my grandparents' milk cows, our place provided subsistence. Even a bad winter meant mostly that by the end of it we were on a very boring diet. The early spring when we lived on pears and green beans was an exception, but not by much. We ate canned fruit until I felt as liquid-boweled as a starling.

We bought staples such as flour, sugar, pinto beans, and oatmeal. The garden was for variety, for canning. Potatoes we grew. I spent many hours picking first the soft grubs and then the adult potato bugs off the plants and dumping them in a mason jar filled with gas or kerosene. Most of the other crops were more bug resistant. Beans and other vegetables needed the weeds hoed out, and melons, potatoes, and plants that grew in hills required hoeing as well. Hoeing weeds is bearable, but forming the hills and rows, breaking up dirt clods with the heavy iron hoe, the preparation of tons of dirt, stooping to pick out rocks and flinging them for the fence lines, is backbreaking. Muscles knot up between your shoulder blades. Blisters form, break, and form in the next layer of skin to break and bleed and collect dirt. Besides being an irritant to the raw flesh, dirt is abrasive, bringing out new blisters. The saying "a tough row to hoe" is not a

lightly meant metaphor for those who've hoed bean rows. My mother
had picked cotton as a child. For her, hoeing a garden was leisure
compared to towing the heavy sacks and slicing her hands to ribbons
on the sharp, dry husks of the cotton boles.

After gardening or sawing wood into lengths with a crosscut, my
father did not mow the lawn with a scythe for exercise. He walked
through, usually in midmorning as soon as the dew was off, swiveling
from the waist, the scythe blade an even distance off the ground.
Each stroke swept the grass into a windrow. This kept the yard somewhat clear of snakes and other pests. The windrows dried by late
afternoon. We raked them into stacks—mulch for the compost or
food for the livestock, if we were keeping any. It may have been while
raking that he heard the peeps of the orphaned bobwhite chicks we
searched out, killing them one by one with our kindness and heavy
shoes.

Meanwhile, evening was coming on. There was sometimes time
for a game of pop-up before the light failed. In dusk like a grainy
photograph, the whippoorwills sang from the stump in the middle of
our yard (third base), so close we could hear the clicking sounds
preceding the call. *Qua Qua, Qu-ip Qu-eel?* they seemed to say close
up, more of a question than a directive. If my father was sharpening
the scythe, the file or whetstone would echo: *quip, quip.* A bit later
and the fireflies started their dance, lighting up, flying straight up,
then flying down to do it over again seconds later. The females syn-
chronized from blades of grass or tree leaves. Things rhymed, harmo-
nized, syncopated like the song of the tree frogs I loved to catch,
pressing their sticky undersides and wondering how they hung onto
trees in thunderstorms.

Out under the eaves of the forest the thousands of lights looked
like an army of hardened soldiers smoking a last cigarette before
attack. A perimeter of stump and low brush surrounded our fence and
had to be cut back. People living along the dirt road kept dogs, lived
back in the woods, were usually armed. They told stories of thefts,

rustling, and events about which they would fall silent when children were about. Many of these were no doubt apocryphal, but there was an atmosphere of watchfulness. When the wills grew quiet, I held my breath. Out in the suddenly expanded night the whirring of the bugs surged and the chorus of tree frogs in the pondside cottonwoods crested.

Up in the unused pasture, that free-range cow who had lost her calf bawled with the pain of a swollen udder. We had no reason to fence the access road, and even if we had, a welded-steel stock fence would have been an unimaginable extravagance. The cow could cost us a night of sleep, but she was neither dangerous nor useful. Such untended stock could have anything from rabies to salmonella to scours to god-only-knows-what. There was no trying to catch or milk her.

The main threat to us was a silent killer. Those who have read Aldo Leopold's "Thinking Like a Mountain" will recognize our enemy. Out in the forest most creatures were nocturnal. The barred owls with their unusual stuttering hoots were looking for squirrels or mice. The bobcats and coyotes sniffed about for rabbits. The rabbits were stalking our vegetables. Rabbits, as any gardener knows, are not timid creatures. They are fast. And ravenous. Desperately trying to pack away the last of the greens, they got so terrified of winter they kept eating until the last instant before running from our dog.

On our ridgeland, any tender young shoot, especially if growing in rows, the weeds carefully hoed away from it, was fair game. The deer were not. In spring the game is thin from winter and birthing. Later the meat of many animals is measled. So, like the cow bellowing in the pasture, like the rabbits and later the raccoons, like the foxes and hawks and owls and weasels and snakes after our chickens, the deer were predators. This is mere peskiness for the suburban gardener who just wants to feel earth in the hands. A pack of coyotes killing a rancher's calf is a bit more serious, though this merely cuts into the profit-loss margin. If a deer walked up to the suburbanite's child and kicked the cereal out of its bowl and began to eat it, or if a rabbit appeared to testify against the rancher receiving a renewal of grazing rights, they would be in somewhat the position we were in vis-à-vis deer and the garden. It was our tenure, our insurance, in the parlance of government, our safety net in a time and place that provided very little other.

I'd like to be a gentleman farmer. Subsistence farming is for those with no option, and commercial farming, as friends of mine have found out, is just that: commercial—heavy industry. Poet and Iowa farmer Michael Carey wrote that "the thing about farming" is that you spend more time killing than nurturing. We put high fences around our garden, hung scraps of cloth on them to discourage deer trying to jump in. We enclosed most of the chicken yard in overhanging wire roof, and placed the coop well inside the fence to discourage aerial and ground attacks. Snakes still got to the eggs. I have a picture of my mother's father, a six-foot man, standing on the raised chicken coop's threshold, a blacksnake's head in his upraised arm. The tail drags the ground.

My parents weren't hunters, but we kept a .22 and box of rifle shells handy. I remember my mother taking aim at a hawk and firing, the red tail feather drifting down to get lost in the trees. My father went hunting one tough winter, but with a .22 he'd have had to be so close he would have been better armed with a rock. Most of the time, we viewed the deer as beautiful scenery, feeding them when we could to bring them near, petting them, and pulling ticks off behind their ears. My father even wrapped a fawn he found tangled in a barbwire fence in his shirt to take it to the game commission. Run to panic by dogs—hopeless. I think the game warden butchered it.

Nurturing is not easy. We got a hundred chicks, reds and leghorns. If I recall correctly, the reds were hardier, the leghorns better eating. We kept them well into spring in a corral around the woodstove where they were never too hot. Sometimes in the morning we would find them huddled in the warmest corner behind the stove for heat.

They were much like a human community in their treatment of the ill. The weak were wise to hide it. A feather out of place would tempt a larger chick to peck to test for frailty. If the first jab drew blood, the rest would poke at this new blemish. Soon the unfortunate chick was mobbed. We kept several in isolation, where they grew even more dispirited and would peep pitifully to assure themselves their tormentors were still nearby.

The stove was the sole source of heat for the chicks and for us. When we heated with wood, I believe we sometimes ran two stoves. The propane range that replaced the kitchen stove heated the house up a lot less in the summer, but left us with one stove for heat.

Soon after we got the range, after the felling of the trees between our house and the road, came electricity. The power-company men had to blast the rocky ground to sink the poles. I watched from the cabin as the boss yelled "fire in the hole," and the men sprinted back. From where I stood, each explosion was a shock in the chest, a splash of red clay and the streamers of flying rocks becoming a pattering rain as the echoes died away. With electricity came the freezer, electric washing machine, and other improvements. They freed my mother from daily fire building, from the old stove-heated irons and the wringer washer. Even with improvements, the image of the cozy, old-fashioned cabin in the frozen woods is a romantic fiction.

I used to think my father was simply a poor cabin builder, or the Ozark second growth was simply too knotty for good cabin building. Having seen badly built ones, I now appreciate that ours was level, and that the corner joints shed water well. Ours was draftier than some, but log cabins are, by definition, cabins: cabanas, huts. The size, construction, and materials of a cabin are not good for keeping in heat. For instance, a cabin roof, especially in the Ozarks where heat is more often an issue than cold, is often a single layer of shingles, tarpaper, or tin. This is what gives it that rustic exposed-beam look. It also means no attic for insulation.

During the bad winter, we could stand facing the woodstove until our pants smoked and still be cold behind. We spent hours turning like chickens on a spit. It was a long walk to the road, and a long drive in the bus. In first grade, I impressed my new friends by kicking the brick wall with my numb foot until the teacher stopped me. She sent for the janitor, and I spent the morning with my foot in a pan of warm water. The feeling came back with interest. It was the first of many pan baths my feet were to get in the coming weeks. At home I'd sit with my back to the stove and my feet in the hot water from the pan on the stove—a happy substitute to the rotisserie maneuver.

My mother invented a game for us to play to get to sleep. We imagined ourselves stuck in a desert on the hottest day we could remember, the thirstiest we had ever been. We cried loud enough to attract the attention of any passersby.

"Water, water. Help."

"Louder! No one will hear you if you can't call louder than that. You don't sound very thirsty. How do you expect to convince anybody that way? They'll think you're cool and comfortable."

Out of such moments, I'm sure, my mother resolved to change her life and ours, to leave behind much that was precious to her to get out of such powerlessness. But not yet. Soon spring came. The surviving chicks were out in a temporary pen. My father was building the coop and the big enclosure, and the weather was heating up. A few months more, and we'd be playing the opposite game, lying with a single sheet over us crying, "It's cold, I can't feel my hands. I want hot chocolate." We were less convincing at this game.

When the chickens were grown and laying, I followed my father to the pen for feeding and egg gathering. The big rooster, king of the coop, took exception to me the first time he saw me, possibly because I was close to his size. The squawking of the hens as my father took their eggs set him off, and he was on me like a schoolyard bully. He grabbed me by my shirtfront, balled up the fabric in both talons, and set about working me over. I ducked my head and put my hands over my face to protect my eyes. He pecked at the top of my head like a woodpecker on a hollow trunk. Meanwhile wings tough and abrasive as a farmer's palm flogged me about the ears.

My father chased him off easily, though he made a couple more feints. I always went into the chicken coop armed afterward, hoping and fearing I would have to use the length of lathe I carried. The hens were no pushovers either. Perhaps they sensed weakness in me the way they would have sensed it in their kind. Maybe I was just too slow. They always got in a good peck as I rummaged under their plumage for eggs. A hen peck is about like the snap from a mousetrap, rarely enough to break skin but enough to make a nice little bruise.

Killing chickens wasn't revenge, just dirty work. My folks usually tied their feet to the clothesline and cut off their heads with a sharp butcher knife. The ax-and-chopping-block number is okay if you want to hold a flopping chicken for a minute and a half as the body flies in every direction. If you want, you can follow it as it runs and half flies, headless, for the woods. With luck it will hit the fence and run blindly against the strands until it has stirred up the drifted leaves, half covering itself, and you have to pick twigs and litter out of the neck hole. Chickens on the clothesline fly almost gracefully, blood arcing out onto the white feathers. Sometimes two of them spun in opposite directions like the whirligigs we used to make out of buttons and string. Seizure.

Nothing is more disgusting than a botched slaughtering job. The worst I remember was watching a bunch of men trying to kill a hog with a .22. The first four or five shots seemed only to annoy it, much like a wasp sting would annoy a man. After the second or third shot, it became obvious the bullets weren't going to penetrate the skull from any distance. A conference followed. Would it be better to wait, leaving the animal in pain, while someone went to borrow a heavier bore rifle? To try capturing the now crazed hog and shoot it through the eye or ear? To try for a heart shot? Someone tried for the heart, but the hog bent around to bite at the wound like a dog biting at fleas. Then they tried to capture it, but it was too big. There was no way of holding it down without taking a chance of shooting one of the men. I left, having no ideas to advance, but heard several more shots, much squealing, and finally silence. When I went past the pen later, I caught a whiff of a unique and lurid odor.

The pig we called Juny was a Berkshire, black with a white stripe. We named her for Juneau, since my mother's sister lived in Alaska while it was applying for statehood. We also kept, at different times, a jersey cow and a goat. The goat was easily the most cantankerous, always getting her foot in the milk pail until my parents began tying her up. She also gave plenty of milk, flavored with whatever she had been eating: milkweed, onions, the labels off tin cans. Alaska made statehood and Juny died. Not allowed outside, I watched through the window while my father tied her feet and opened her jugular with two strokes of the butcher knife. The only squeals were her cries of indignation at being tied up.

From several lengths of rough wood slab discarded by a local sawmill, we built a smokehouse. Hickory from our own woods smoked the meat. Also from the hickory, my father saved a long twisted branch shaped perfectly for a scythe handle—three bends in a recurve like a bow. Perhaps because I was in school, I don't remember the business end of the Juny episode—the dismembering, the skinning, debristling, plucking, disemboweling—only the fine, rich smell of the smokehouse and, vaguely, my parents washing blood off a handsaw.

My parents were the most peaceful people I ever met. They distinguished fighting, aggression, and other violence from self-defense from an early age. I think it bothered them to kill animals. In such country, however, one lives with the products of one's living. One either buries the offal or leaves it for the animals—pets and wild. We dug a pit and built our outhouse over it, and when it was full, we tore down the outhouse and covered the pit. Down in the woods was the dump. Everything that couldn't be burned or composted—mostly cans—went to a ravine where it served as riprap. There were old bedsprings from earlier inhabitants, real tin cans.

Some animal-rights activists argue that if people had to butcher their own meat, they'd soon turn vegetarian. Aside from the fact that most people in the world as a whole *do* have to butcher at least some of their own meat, I like the core of the argument. If most of the urbanized people the statement aims at had to be responsible for hand-producing a substantial portion of their own food, they'd have a much better idea of what it costs in time, energy, and dirty, violent work. After spading under a dozen or so acres of flowers and hauling and spreading manure or compost to plant, say, corn or beans; repeatedly hoeing back the weeds (that is, indigenous flora); fencing out, trapping, and killing or shooing away the indigenous fauna; irrigating; harvesting the crop amid clouds of itching dust; and shucking, pealing, hulling, milling, pulverizing, or otherwise processing it into flour, mush, porridge, hominy, or grits—after this, most people find killing and butchering a chicken just another not particularly offensive chore.

Euthanasia was another responsibility. When our dog Shadow disturbed either a nest of black hornets or a copperhead, his face swelled up like a bulldog's. His jowls hung slack and draped with slobber. We could have found a neighbor with a truck to take him twenty painfully rough miles to the nearest veterinarian. Or tied him up, ignoring his howls until he either recovered or asphyxiated. My father shot him.

Travelers in Third World countries and Indian reservations often remark on the cruelty of poor people to their dogs. Yet, when I worked for a veterinary clinic, I saw suburbanites weep and refuse to let the vets unhook their jaundiced dog or cat from an IV until the victim's liver burst. Keep your eyes open as you drive past the outskirts of your town or city. On the freeway margins, animals clipped like topiary shrubs fight the crows for roadkill. The difference is between people who do and do not have to live with the consequences of their actions. For most Americans (not just city folk, but the increasingly automated farmers and ranchers) the dump, scrap

yard, sewage plant, slaughterhouse, and animal shelter are mostly out
of sight and out of mind.

A Park Service brochure put out a few years ago listed the indigenous animals one was likely to see along the Current River. Listed
with weasels, beavers, raccoons, and deer, the Ozark hound stood
out. I asked the ranger whether the dogs had truly gone feral. He
looked embarrassed, like someone who often has to explain the mis-
takes of superiors to the public.

"I wish they hadn't put that in there," he said. "They're just
hunting dogs running loose, till we round them up when they get too
thick around the campgrounds. They're more trouble than anything
else. I guess whoever wrote that thought it would seem more authen-
tic if they gave them a name."

They look like dogs I had, a lot of beagle in the calico coats, and
various other types of hound. The occasional one sports a flag tail and
feathering from having a retriever somewhere in the woodpile. Registered breeds are not important to most backwoods hunters. In this
they're like the horse owners with what's called an Ozark walker or
Missouri trotter. "It's just a good all-round horse," someone might
say, meaning it can pull a wagon and is saddlebroke with a good stride
for trail riding.

Besides a couple of good dogs, I had one that had to go on a one-
way hunting trip. Miney was the third child. Her name was a constant reminder of her birth order, younger sister of Eenie and Meenie.
If there was a Moe, I never saw it. Miney was a runt, and was owly her
whole short life, but I liked her. She lured me into the strange,
narrow, upside-down world under the cabin for companionship. She
was a good watchdog, after her fashion, which was to bark constantly
unless someone was coming. Even in her sleep under the cabin, she
would keep up a yipping sort of sleep talk.

She was the only dog our quiet neighbor on his surefooted walker

couldn't fool. Usually we'd walk out the door into his shadow as he
sat on his horse—inside our yard. Then the dogs would bark, as
surprised as us but putting a good face on it. Miney would be quiet
for several minutes before we became suspicious, but when we looked
out, there he was.

Or there he wasn't. Miney was sometimes quiet because someone
else was coming, or deer were passing in the woods, or a hawk was
circling the henhouse. She was afraid of everything. She was such a
good watchdog that for a long time we thought she was normal, if a
little quiet, and looked outside when she barked. Sometimes she was
so observant we never did see what it was she wasn't barking at.
Visitors never did say so, but it seemed as if the sudden silences and
our rushing to the windows to look out made them nervous.

I was playing with Miney on the back steps when it happened. The
game might be called teasing with a stick or pull-the-ears or blow-
on-the-nose-until-you-sneeze. Miney, unlike most dogs, was nervous
around children. Whether because she was jumpy from my playing or
simply displaying her usual cowardice, she attacked when I stepped on
her foot. It wasn't a prolonged attack. She snapped with a growling
bark unlike her usual yapping. Then I was walking down along the
fence crying, my lip so swollen I could see it. Miney tried to lick my
face. The bite closed up without stitches, and the only visible traces
are two purple spots that appear when I get cold. My father shot her
that afternoon.

Paisoni (pronounced pie-ZONE-ey) was, in the parlance of Park
Service brochures, an Ozark hound. He was mostly beagle. His name
was a corruption of *paesano*. The neighbor who named him, the
solitary bachelor who kept a rock pile outside his house for his friends
the snakes, had served in Italy during World War II. According to
him, "Piezoney means friend in eye-talian." Paisoni picked up no love
of snakes from his early home. He would kill them on sight. He also
brought dozens of box turtles home, but he could not do them much
harm. He would chew at one for an hour and draw the slightest bit of

blood at the corner of the carapace. He'd come dragging one across the yard, dropping it, dragging it, yipping as it poked its head out to nip at his paws. My mother drove him off his prey with rocks as big as the turtles. She tied him up until they'd got away, but half an hour later he'd come dragging them back. He chased rabbits, squirrels, cows, and pigs.

Cows and pigs no longer run semiwild in the Ozarks. It's better for the land. Without predators to keep the populations down, only disease or lack of food from overgrazing could control them. Cattle suffer on open range. Hogs, quick-witted and omnivorous, soon revert to a tusked advertisement for Gordon's Gin. Pigs may have been the most dangerous animals loose in the woods, but it was wolves I was on the lookout for. I often went to my grandmother's for milk—about a mile along the old access road that ran up to and then alongside the tram road. If attacked, I planned to buy my escape with my miniature milk can, a half-gallon pail with a tight-fitting lid. Never mind that there hadn't been wolves in the Ozarks in the memory of the oldest folks alive. Strangely, the fear left not even a memory when I reached the set of stairs that crossed the fence on my grandmother's property.

Known as a fence jack, these stairs were common in the Ozarks. Fences are difficult to build and maintain. A gate, with the necessarily heavy gatepost that toggles back and forth in its hole, invites frost heave to push it out of the ground. Another piece of rusticity preserved in the countryside (now with an eye to the tourist trade) is the zigzag split-rail fence. On rocky ground that heaves out fence posts but provides plenty of logs, this fence, sitting on top of the ground, is a good compromise. It's made of split rails crisscrossed at the ends and nailed or notched together. They are self-supporting. The difficulty is in making a gate, since anything less than a full circle would weaken the chain. Again, the obvious solution is a fence jack.

Mark Twain described a fence jack as something built by people too lazy to build a proper gate. He was not particularly generous in

his portrayals of lower Missouri and Arkansas hill-country inhabitants. Maybe this was because he dealt with townspeople along the
Mississippi, who serviced riverboats and were subject to the dilatory
influence of their wealth. Another of Twain's literary offenses was his
slavish following of fashion in judging horseflesh. What he describes
as the plow horses ridden by farmers may be the first literary refer-
ence to what later (and more public-relations-minded) generations
would call the Ozarks fox-trotter.

The very fence I crossed on my way to my grandmother's was the
site of the only courting story I remember about my parents. I have
photographs of them from the period, very attractive young people,
my mother tall and slender with nearly platinum blond hair. After her
hair fell out when she was pregnant with me, it all came back dark. A
picture of my father standing on a rock outcropping wearing a tur-
tleneck sweater made me want one when I first saw it. They made his
neck itch, he said, and he was glad they went out of style. I still think
he made it look good. A face as delicate as the sensitive pea; touch it
and it folds in on itself. I look at the photo and wonder if, on a trip to
New York in his youth to have tests for his epilepsy, he couldn't have
been discovered by a modeling agency.

A photo from St. Louis: we're all in suits, Dad in the brown (I
imagine) double-breasted, Mom in one of those square-shouldered,
straight-skirted beauties, and me in the effete Buster Brown. For
ridge-runners, we cleaned up pretty well. Without the kid that young
couple might have had some fun, might have raised some hell. They
could have used it.

But, no. They weren't the type. They'd arrange to be walking with
friends along the fence line afternoons, and run into one another. On
one of these outings, my father had ripped out the seat of his trousers
on the fence. He was going home to change when my mother came
past. According to her, he stayed to talk longer than usual, until they
both ran out of things to say. When he left, he backed over the fence
jack, still talking, and down the path into the woods, waving and

smiling. Finally, he turned and she could see the flash of white in the large tear as he bounded into the woods like a whitetail deer.

I can't look at those photos without bitterness. This is what my mother was trying to remind me with her version of the beatitudes: "Don't harden your heart." Hard advice when I consider those young people with even their delicate, strange beauty against them. It's a wonder worse didn't happen to them than did. The meek *do* inherit the earth, don't they?—at least, after the powerful have had their way with it?

This is not The Way. Back to the *Tao Te Ching:*

> The highest good is to be like water.
> Water can sustain the ten thousand things
> without ever competing with them.
> Because it inhabits the low places most people scorn
> it is always close to the Path.
>
> Search for the highest good:
> in dwelling, the good lies in the land;
> in the mind, the good is depth;
>   in giving, being humane;
> in speaking, the good is trust;
>   in governing, order;
> in projects, the good is ability;
>   in action, timeliness.
>
> Only that which does not contend
> is without blame.

Arriving at my grandmother's with my milk pail, I'd have graham crackers and milk—whole milk from her cows with perhaps one skimming of cream taken off. Thick rich milk, it was relatively low in calcium, being from cows that grazed ridgeland pastures. Sometimes

she would send me home with an extra jar, depending on how pro-
ductive the cows had been. Sometimes my parents and our nearby
neighbors the Vales would save up cream and I would churn butter.
The churn consisted of crank-driven paddles in a large jar, a device
more like an ice cream maker than like wooden churns one sees in
museums. The Vales also made cottage cheese, strong, grassy-tasting
curds I ate with cinnamony, chunky applesauce from their trees.

The land was a rich provider most of the time, rich in food, in
companionship, in imagery for my imagination. The imagery was a
handicap when I left the sanctuary of my grandmother's house to
return through the shady woods to the cabin. Surely the rustling
brush on either side of the road hid the lone wolf, waiting for me to
be out of hearing of both houses.

Real danger, like the highest good of the *Tao,* is usually duller than
we like to imagine it. Even pigs were little danger. Insects were more
threat. We lit smudge pots of smelly coal oil on evenings of no breeze
when it was too hot to go inside, sunset through dusk. Chiggers
blistered our skin and fed on the dissolved tissues, the mosquitoes
worried our faces and ears, and the ticks—though they did not then
carry fever—attached themselves in every crevice. Under these constant attacks, Dave developed a painful furuncle under his arm, a
large, boil-like swelling that had to be lanced. Every summer day
ended with the exhaustive and embarrassing full-body search.

Within the confines of our life, strength and danger both were
understated. Still extant were not only timber rattler and the screaming puma, but also the copperhead, the black widow, the brown
recluse, the cottonmouth. Not fatal, these latter, but not to be ignored. Here also are cures for something bigger that threatens to
overwhelm not just these low-lying islands of biological and cultural
diversity. You need not believe in the efficacy of stump water, water
witching, or the plug of tobacco kept under the lip as cure for a
cancerous lip lesion. I don't. But something like a magical circle of
symbols has given me vision at many points in my life. Many of those

images are most clearly drawn in the red dirt of this part of the world. Like our families, our home soils stay with us whether we ever return to drink at the home wells or not. That soil is fertile in ways the county extension agent's charts will never show.

On visits to the area, I have not looked up my relatives. I don't stop to introduce myself to childhood classmates who still run family businesses or farms. What I find most hopeful is not the new business made possible by tourism, nor even the preservation of the folk culture in which I peripherally participated, but the resurrection of the land itself. The soil rebuilds under the growing forest, and hillside vistas of ragged growth become luxuriant. The pine seedlings I helped plant grow into twenty- and thirty-foot trees. Water fouled by logging and mining runs clear again.

Yet I would like to think that what I value, the shy, deferential character of most of the people I remember, remains.

As a child, I was busy planting and digging up many things—pines, rocks, images. Children always have their heads down at the ground or up to the sky, and very seldom on human affairs. In 1959 or 1960, my mother and father separated, and I did not see the Ozarks for more than twenty-five years. One impression I preserved was of summer's intense light, the hazy bronze halo that refused to describe the sun. I imagined one could candle eggs by that light. Researchers suspect that Stradivari held up violin soundboards to sunlight to identify the denser grain and plane it thinner for a uniform resonance.

I tried it on snake eggs. In a sunbaked part of our yard, garter snakes laid their eggs. The clayey soil retained so much heat that a fog sprang up around the house after a rainfall. The place was perfect for incubation—except for the presence of a prepubescent boy who was just beginning to wonder about birth. These wonderings and stirrings were as hazy and diffuse as the light. I'd seen the pigs rut, vaguely troubled at their fleshiness, knowing my fascination was nothing I wanted to ask my parents about. When I asked my mother what my belly button was, she had said it was where I was fed when I was growing inside her from an egg to a baby. I imagined myself to have been a sort of dimpled bean, a skin-covered seed.

This was what I saw when I dug up the snake eggs, a cache of skin beans about the shape and size of white grapes or the gooseberries we picked along the fencerows. Making the OK sign around one egg with my thumb and forefinger, I could use the sun as a candling light. Inside the skin, like a heart beating, I saw or imagined the wavy line of a snake thrashing in the light. It could have been the line I created trying to draw a tree or map the creek. The image I retain is an animated stick figure, a man with no arms. My thought's embryo or the snake's, it stayed centered in its orange ocean, never getting any closer to the shore, a zigzag, a river, a process, a stream of earth momentarily suspended in a circle of water.

Acknowledgments

"Magic" first appeared in *Georgia Review* 48:1 (spring 1994).

"My Father Cannot Draw a Man," quoted from *Enter Dark Stranger* by William Trowbridge (University of Arkansas Press, 1989), is used by permission of the author.

The author wishes to acknowledge the assistance of the University Committee on Research at the University of Nebraska at Omaha for a Summer Fellowship in 1989, which allowed work on this project to begin.